DUEL IN THE DARK

They agreed on at least one thing:

Hitler: 'The spirit of the British people enables it to carry through to victory any struggle that it once enters upon, no matter how long...or however great the sacrifice.'

Churchill: (visiting bombed-out civilians): 'I see the spirit of an unconquerable people.'

DUEL IN THE DARK

Peter Townsend

ARROW BOOKS

Arrow Books Limited
62-65 Chandos Place, London WC2N 4NW

An imprint of Century Hutchinson Limited

London Melbourne Sydney Auckland
Johannesburg and agencies throughout
the world

First published by Harrap Ltd 1986
Arrow edition 1988

Printed and bound in Great Britain by
Anchor Brendon Limited, Tiptree, Essex

ISBN 0 09 953230 1

CONTENTS

ILLUSTRATIONS

Rescue

Damaged ward at Forest Gate Hospital
New-born babies being evacuated from a hospital
A patient being rescued at St Matthew's Hospital
Nurses retrieving bedding
Damaged wing of St Thomas's Hospital
Digging for survivors off the Strand
Bomb at the Bank Underground Station
Rescuers find a survivor at Budge Row
Tea from the Salvation Army
A wounded boy is rescued
A woman victim is resuscitated
Farringdon Market rocket damage

The aftermath

Bombed buildings in Goswell Road, E1
Fallen masonry on the High Altar, St Paul's
A bomb crater revealing the crypt, St Paul's
A view from the roof of St Paul's
Madame Tussaud's, Marylebone Road
Street scene, Balham
Great Hall of the Guildhall after bombing
St Mary Le Bow, Cheapside
Liverpool Street Station
Central Criminal Court
Churchill surveys the damage at the Commons
Piccadilly, London, showing bomb damage

Life goes on

Shoppers at a damaged bakery
A couple bombed out of their home
King George VI and Queen Elizabeth at Hendon
Londoners asleep in the tube
Miss Ellen Wilkinson on a tour of inspection
Suburban homes the morning after a raid
Feeding the pigeons as usual in Trafalgar Square
An Eastender at his bombed house

PREFACE

This book is a natural sequel to *Duel of Eagles*, in which I described the events culminating in 1940 in the Battle of Britain (the first decisive battle ever fought in the air) when the RAF day-fighters defeated the Luftwaffe, and thus put an end to Hitler's aim of eliminating Britain from the war and leaving him master of Europe.

The day battle over, the Germans switched to a relentless night-bombing offensive whose object was to subdue the British into surrender. Göring, the Luftwaffe chief, announced the 'progressive annihilation' of London and British industrial and harbour towns.

The day-fighter squadron, No. 85, that I had led during the day battle was in the autumn of 1940 abruptly assigned (as were half a dozen others) to the role of a night-fighter squadron. I tell the story here of how we in the night defences — in the face of formidable technical and weather problems — tried, with little success at first, to help stem the nine-months-long German night onslaught. This was the 'Night Blitz' — when Britain, alone with her loyal Commonwealth, and the few brave, invaluable remnants of her allied forces — kept fighting on at home as well as on many foreign fronts.

I am deeply indebted to the following persons and institutions who helped so readily in my researches:

Air Commodore Henry Probert, Head of the Historical Branch, Ministry of Defence, and his staff, notably Sebastian Cox, an expert on the Luftwaffe;

Andrew Orgill, Librarian of the Adastral Library, and his staff;

The Imperial War Museum;

The Public Records Office;

Oberst Hans-Joachim Weste, German air attaché in Paris, who kindly put me in touch with

Herr Berthold Krüger, president of the Kampfgeschwader 2 Comrades Association, who in turn put me on the trail of Herr Martin Mummer, observer of the Dornier 217 I intercepted one dark night in February 1941. My letter to him was apologetic. I felt sorry for the harm I had done to Mummer and his companions. No reply was forthcoming.

Patrick and Penny Langrishe kindly lent me the wartime diary of their uncle, the late Ronald Horley. It was a source of inspiration, both literary and artistic.

The wide connections of Pat Barnard, Director of the Military Gallery, Bath, were invaluable, particularly as he led me to Ray Callow and his brother Johnny, to whom I am grateful for giving me many hours of their time, so that I could form a lively picture of how Londoners 'took it' during those long winter nights of the 'Blitz'.

Although the incident occurred after the period covered by this book, Mrs 'Dinkie' Kiddley helped my understanding by recalling vividly her memories of the disastrous bombing of Sandhurst Road School, where she was a seven-year-old pupil.

I am most grateful to Roy Minton, of Harraps, for his helpful suggestions; and finally to Dana Noyé and my daughter Françoise for typing my manuscript.

I feel undying admiration for the people of London and all the other blitzed cities and towns of Britain. It was they who, bare-handed, did more than we armed men to keep Hitler out of our island.

PETER TOWNSEND
June 1986

1

TROPICAL NIGHTS

Night had fallen on Singapore. In those tropical latitudes the sun, blazing overhead all day, sank swiftly at eventide below the horizon, and day changed abruptly into night. In the brief half-hour of dusk, I had made a few 'circuits and bumps' to get accustomed to the flare-path — a row of half a dozen buckets, spaced out over as many hundred yards, containing kerosene in which a kind of wick, like a mop, was immersed. They burned with an orange flame which trailed away in a wispy cloud of black smoke.

Each one of these crude flares was minded by a Tamil boy, as black as the night itself. His job was to stoke the fire. Sometimes an aeroplane landing too close to the flare-path would fan the flares into a wild blaze and send the Tamil boys scurrying off to safety.

Now it was dark, I took off again. This time on my first 'night solo', piloting a Vickers Vildebeest, a big biplane as ugly as its African namesake. In the open cockpit, the pilot's sole protection was a small windscreen.

The Vildebeest's huge propeller, a masterpiece of woodwork carved out of laminated mahogany, churned the air, dragging the aircraft along at a comfortable cruising speed of 95 mph. In a dive you dared not exceed 140 mph, otherwise you were likely to continue diving minus the tail-unit. But the Vildebeest, within its limits, was a trusty friend, for which (though bred as a fighter-pilot) I formed a deep affection.

Climbing away into the starry, purple sky, I rejoiced as much in the immense feeling of puissance and solitude as in the smell of the warm night air. In Malay kampongs and Chinese villages lights flickered; they were cooking the evening meal, and mixed odours of grilled fish and spices and burning charcoal wafted up until they pervaded my cockpit. Some way south the lights of Singapore twinkled brightly. Above, stars crowded the heavens, their customary brilliance slightly faded in the pale light of the rising moon. I flew on into the midst of the night, marvelling at that multitude of celestial bodies and feeling like an extra-terrestrial body myself, at one with them.

These were dream conditions for night-flying. With the stars above, and the lighted earth beneath, you at least could tell that you were the right way up. In those days — and nights — men flew like birds; people sometimes called us birdmen, even intrepid birdmen. That made us laugh, though in fact we preferred to fly as the birds do, with the horizon before us separating earth and sky, rather than to concentrate anxiously on the 'turn and bank indicator', a dial in the centre of the dashboard whose two needles wobbled uncertainly. This instrument, with your compass and altimeter (graded in hundreds of feet), was supposed to help you in poor visibility to fly straight and level. It was a hateful little instrument, which perpetually conveyed the impression that your aircraft was erring in every direction but the right one. But give us the natural horizon and we flew like the birds.

That night in Singapore was the 1st of September 1936. I was twenty-one and supremely happy with my life as a pilot, dangerous though it was and far from home. Singapore was ten days' flying from London. My first night-flight, alone at the controls, was a new adventure in flying, the career which, since the age of fourteen, I had firmly decided to follow.

No one could force you to be a pilot; you became one out of love, of a passion for flying. While in the exclusive Tanglin Club or at Raffles Hotel you might spend a blissful evening in the select company of some well-bred daughter of the British community or at the Happy World, in the arms of a lissom Chinese hostess, dancing away the hours, but your first love was for your ugly Vildebeest, with its oily reek and the emotions it provided in plenty. A pilot more in love with a girl than his aircraft grew broody, and lost the taste for the risks of his trade.

Flying was for me pure romance. The technical aspect, though inevitable, was secondary. I took to the working of the engine without too much trouble because it was full of amusing names: big-ends and little-ends, crankshafts and camshafts, poppet valves and sprockets, splines and pinions and push-rods. They made music, as did the steady rhythm of the Bristol Pegasus engine itself, as its 650 'horses' turned that great wooden windmill in front.

We trusted the engine implicitly, flying as we always were over the sea and jungle. Occasionally a sparking-plug would blow out, but the 'Peggy', puffing like a steam-engine, would bring us safely home.

The technicalities of radio, on the other hand, were for ever to remain beyond my understanding. As an eighteen-year-old pupil pilot I had listened intently, but comprehending nothing, to our diminutive signals flight-sergeant. When at the end of one lecture he inquired 'Any questions?' I quickly thought up some unlikely electronic hypothesis and put it to him, asking for an explanation.

'That's enough from you, smarty,' he snapped. Thereafter it was only in the most simplistic terms that I could grasp the basics of the intriguing mysteries of radio. Meanwhile the important thing was to know the right button to push, and thus benefit gratuitously from that marvel of man's inventive genius. I mention this to reassure the reader who may be as ignorant as I am in the field of electronics, which were to become a vital factor in the air war.

Both before and during the German air raids on Britain, both sides were vying with each other in a separate theatre of war, the 'Wizard War' (as Mr Winston Churchill, a self-confessed novice on the subject, called it).

The Vildebeest did not normally carry a radio set; we could communicate with no one, either in the heavens above or on the earth beneath. Only by day could we make hand signs — sometimes rude ones — to a near-by aircraft. By night when we set forth in flight or squadron strength across the sharky waters of the South China Sea for a practice torpedo attack against some complaisant liner or naval vessel we, the wing-men, still carried no radio. On such special occasions, however, a W/T (wireless telegraphy) set and operator were installed in our flight commanders' aircraft. The 'Wireless Op' could communicate with base in Morse Code. Our job — not always an easy one — was to follow the navigation lights (red on the left wing-tip, green on the right) of our leader's aircraft.

The target ship located (this, with all its lights burning, was no great problem), an obliging accomplice, specially designated in our formation, would drop a flare, or maybe several. Down went our flight commander, his wing-men following. The torpedo, carried between the wheels of the fixed undercarriage, had, of course, a dummy warhead. We would 'put her in' at 25 feet above the surface. This somewhat hazardous task accomplished, we would then look up, searching among the myriad stars for two special ones — the red and green lights of our leader. With luck we would join up with him and follow him home. Otherwise we would have to make it back to base alone on a compass course. Fortunately, the lights of Singapore, of the Happy World and other fun-spots, burned late and were visible — at least in good weather — from afar. Disregarding our compass, and with a passing thought for an evening off duty on the morrow, we would steer towards them.

Such was the uncomplicated nature of radio and air navigation in the mid-thirties in that distant outpost of Empire. If not highly technical, it was warmly human.

2

'THIS CURSED, HELLISH INVENTION'

I returned home, to Tangmere in Sussex, in mid-1937. It was there, two years earlier as a twenty-year-old pilot officer, that I had joined No. 1 Fighter Squadron. This time I went to No. 43, No. 1's sister.

Little appeared to have changed. The usual crop of hay had been taken off the airfield, a broad meadow unspoilt by any runway, where sheep now peacefully grazed. The two fighter squadrons' gleaming Hawker Fury biplanes stood lined up on the tarmac: their fuselage and top wing decorated with the squadron's markings: a flaming red triangle for No. 1, a black-and-white chequerboard for No. 43. Yet there was one unusual feature. The place was full of new young faces, many more than in the past. Moreover, Tangmere was no longer purely a fighter station; a coastal reconnaissance squadron, No. 217, with twin-motor Avro Ansons, had come to roost there. The RAF's expansion was now urgently under way, in face of the German Luftwaffe's enormous and ever-growing strength. As long ago as 1934 Mr Churchill, then MP for Epping, had warned Parliament 'We are vulnerable as we have never been before . . . . This cursed, hellish invention and development of air power has revolutionized our position.' At the time he had faced jeers and insults: 'Medieval baron! warmonger!' Now people were listening to him. He sat on the Air Defence Research Committee, and knew better than anyone Britain's urgent need to modernize and strengthen her air defences. The most pressing need of all was to devise a scientific method of detecting hostile aircraft approaching our shores. Crude experiments had been made in 1934 with two huge sound-locators near the Kent coast, but a year later Dr (later Sir) Robert Watson-Watt, already known as a brilliant physicist, came up with the answer: high-frequency radio beams (actually discovered some four decades earlier). Watson-Watt immediately went to work on a system with the cover-name of Radio Detection (RDF, soon to be called radar). The building began of twenty 'Chain Home' (CH) radar stations, stretching along the coast, from the Orkneys to the Isle of Wight.

It was one thing to detect hostile aircraft at long range, another to guide our fighters to within sighting distance of them. This side of the business was entrusted to Fighter Command's new chief, Air Marshal Sir Hugh Dowding. He set up a telephonic network linking the coastal radar stations with the operations room at Fighter Command headquarters, thence to each of its six Group headquarters, and from them down to each of their Sector operations rooms. Thus the enemy 'plots', first seen on the coastal stations' radar screen and reported by telephone to Fighter Command, could be replotted a few moments later on the operations map at the Sector station where the fighter squadrons waited, ready to go, guided to the 'hostile' by radio-telephone (RT) by the Sector controller. Though yet far from complete, the system was unique.

Five radar stations out of the twenty planned were on watch when Hitler's Wehrmacht, with the Luftwaffe thundering overhead, invaded Austria in March 1938. Churchill, the watchdog of Britain's defences, again loudly voiced his increasing concern. Britain and her allies, he roundly declared in Parliament, must choose either to submit to Hitler or else take effective measures against him.

The measures so far taken in the realm of air defence were derisive. Britain possessed but a quarter of her essential coastal radar stations. Her fighter squadrons were too few, and equipped with old-fashioned biplanes. Delivery of modern anti-aircraft guns had hardly begun; to fill the gap, out-of-date three-inch guns were being hastily refurbished — some, it was said, had been commandeered from the Imperial War Museum. Searchlights and barrage balloons were in short supply, as were the trained crews needed to operate them.

Barely six months after Hitler's rape of Austria, Britain and her ally France came to the verge of war with Germany, this time over Hitler's threat to liquidate Czechoslovakia as a political entity. But neither of the allies, despite their protests, had the stomach for a showdown with the Nazi dictator. The Luftwaffe chief Göring was talking of the English skies being darkened by masses of Luftwaffe bombers as they flew on to deliver the 'knockout blow' against London.

The British air minister Kingsley Wood was predicting half a million civilian casualties in the first three weeks of air attack. Cowed by the menacing Luftwaffe, the British cabinet authorized prime minister Neville Chamberlain to negotiate with Hitler. He and the French prime minister Daladier met the Fuehrer at Munich. On landing back at Croydon, London's airport, on 30 September, the smiling Chamberlain held aloft a sheet of white paper signed by Hitler. It guaranteed, he told the rapturous crowd, 'peace in our time'. It also meant, though Chamberlain did not say so, the sacrifice of Czechoslovakia to the rapacious Nazi warlord.

Relief in Britain was heartfelt. From the cabinet down to the man in the street, the fear of air attack was very real, though time would prove that both Kingsley Wood and Göring were wildly exaggerating the effect of aerial bombardment — unless gas were used. This was always a possibility. However, the truth was that our air defences were in no shape to prevent heavy air-raids, had the Luftwaffe launched them.

Barely a hundred AA guns could be found to defend London, let alone our ports and industrial cities. Searchlights were equally poor in numbers and performance; both they and the guns depended for aiming on sound-locators which were practically useless against fast-flying aircraft. Balloon barrages were not yet dense enough to dissuade low-flying bombers. The coastal radar chain afforded only partial cover, and did not yet perform reliably.

Finally, Fighter Command, Britain's first line of defence, possessed 750 fighters. Only ninety of them were Hurricanes, the latest — and redoubtable — model, but the Hurricane's eight guns froze up above 15,000 feet. The Spitfire was not yet ready. The rest of the fighters were a mixed lot of out-of-date biplanes, like our Furies; we ourselves, once part of an élite force of interceptors, could not now even catch the Luftwaffe's more speedy Heinkel and Dornier bombers. Global figures, moreover, are misleading; only about half of that motley force of 750 fighters would be serviceable — fit to fly — at any one time.

And our night-fighters? It was by no means sure that the Luftwaffe would not bomb under cover of night (as indeed it was eventually to do). Night-fighting was literally as different from day-fighting as night is from day. Special radar equipment, both in the fighter aircraft and for the use of ground control, were essential (save for the odd fluke) to successful interception at night. Specially trained pilots were equally necessary. In none of these requirements did any specialized night-fighter force exist. In 43 and 1 Squadrons, we joked about night-flying. The night was made for love, as the song went, not for flying. Only fools and owls flew at night, and anyway our Furies were declared unsuitable for night-flying. So we were not bothered.

3

THIS HAPPY BREED

If the Munich crisis found Britain's (not to mention France's) air defences still so pitifully feeble, the people of Britain — not for the last time — demonstrated their will to defy Germany, and especially Hitler. The British public, we of Fighter Command included, could not yet believe that 'Adolf', who, with his proud strutting, his screeching voice and wild gestures, was taken for a kind of music-hall character, could seriously upset our easy-going, enjoyable way of life. 'Adolf' had no lack of imitators who made us rock with laughter.

Göring, with his portly figure, his comic-opera uniforms and lavish display of decorations, seemed better suited to vaudeville. But his threats of annihilation from the air did, after all, strike home.

It was the British citizen, the man in the street, his wife and children, who stood to suffer most from the 'knock-out blow' of explosive, fire and possibly gas promised by that other Nazi warlord, with his dreaded Luftwaffe. At no time did the British feel more that their home was their castle, nor were they ever more determined to defend it. In the six months between Austria and Munich half a million men and women came forward as volunteers for the Civil Defence Service, as air-raid wardens, firemen, ambulance drivers, despatch riders, telephonists, rescue workers and the like.

The appeasement of Hitler at Munich, humiliating as it was, gave Britain nearly a year, the 'Year of Salvation', to press forward ever more urgently with her defences, including civil defence (Air Raid Precautions, as it was simply called) against attack from the air. The Munich crisis, when Hyde Park and other pleasant London parks and commons were disfigured by hastily dug trenches and thirty-five million gasmasks were handed out, brought the British people abruptly face to face with the dreadful reality of war — total war, in which the civil population would be in the front line.

Six months after Munich, in March 1939, the armed hordes of the Fuehrer (with the Luftwaffe, as usual, thundering overhead) marched without opposition into Czechoslovakia. Hitler declared: 'Czechoslovakia has ceased to exist.'

In Britain a month later, conscription — always considered an affront to our liberties — compelled twenty-year-olds to join up; their numbers were steadily swelled by volunteers outside the age category who came flocking to the colours. Yet another half-million men and women volunteered for civil defence — 'ordinary people' who in the coming hours of darkness, unarmed save with their courage, were to prove themselves far from ordinary.

One such volunteer was Johnny Callow, a Londoner from Woolwich. Churchill had described London as the biggest target in the world, and likened the capital to a fat cow, tethered and awaiting the slaughter. London's number one military target was Woolwich Arsenal, a huge complex of munition factories covering ten square miles with its own railway service and even its own little navy, for it was traversed by canals giving on to the south bank of the river Thames. The Arsenal was six miles as the crow flies downstream from that ancient Norman stronghold the Tower of London, which since Plantagenet times had served as a depot (and still does) for weapons. Woolwich, originally a fishing-village, succeeded the Tower, and, well before Trafalgar and Waterloo, it assumed the role and the title of the Royal Arsenal.

Johnny's father, Henry Callow, got his first job driving the pair of horses which pulled, at full gallop, the fire-engine of the neighbouring borough, Southwark. Then followed a spell as groom to the colonel commanding the Royal Regiment of Artillery, the 'Gunners', whose home — like that of the Royal Engineers, the 'Sappers' — is at Woolwich, the 'Garrison Town'. In time Henry forsook the colonel's horses for the white horses of the high seas. He joined the Merchant Navy as a stoker.

Young marriages and large families were the tradition among Londoners, though they lived, most of them, in extreme poverty. Barely out of his teens, Henry Callow married, and he and his Irish wife, Mary-Anne, began to found their family during Henry's leave ashore. By the outbreak of war in 1914 they already had three children, Johnny being one of them. He was four when his father went off to sea again as an engine-room greaser in the Royal Navy. Back from the war, Henry Callow signed on again in the Merchant Navy. He and Mary-Anne increased their family. Ray, their last and tenth child (two had died in infancy), was born in 1927, about the time I made my first flight as a thirteen-year-old schoolboy and started along the road which would lead me to the Battle of Britain and the night battle which followed — the 'Night Blitz'.

At that time also, Johnny — now seventeen — was set on becoming a professional ballroom dancer. Though he had the warm heart of his father, he was physically the very opposite — short and spare and soft of speech. A natural athlete, he first proved himself during the autumn nights of 1915 when German zeppelins began bombing London, looking like silver sausages floating in the searchlight beams while a few anti-aircraft gun-bursts crackled around them. Johnny's job was to run round shinning up the lamp-posts and pull the little ring on the end of a chain which doused the gas-light. While this impromptu blackout proceeded a policeman would cycle along the streets, a notice in large letters attached to his back saying 'TAKE COVER'. There was in fact no effective cover to take, other than the occasional basement like the one beneath the Tabernacle church in Beresford Street. Even then, people were in no hurry to go underground.

Johnny, like all little boys in Woolwich, belonged to a gang —

21

no gang of young criminals, but a little band of friends united in their love for sport and fun, with a harmless dose of mischief thrown in, and ever willing to earn a penny or two for services rendered. Most of the gang were sons of market traders — 'squareheads' as they were called, not because they were dim-witted (far from it) but because their stalls were ranged in Beresford Square. Johnny earned more pennies from strapping down the horses of the costermongers who drove their carts up to Covent Garden market where they bought their produce. So small was he that he had to climb on to a stool to brush the horses' manes, except when it came to old Ben who obligingly lowered his head.

Johnny, like his Irish mother, was a Catholic. Daily he walked the two miles to St Peter's Catholic school, and another two more miles home in the evening. His parents had not the money to buy him a bicycle or a bus ticket; poverty was the common lot of most Londoners. But they survived, and later triumphed, on humour, courage and mutual help. The Callows' front door, like everyone else's, was left on the latch, and never locked; anyone could lift the latch by pulling on the string which protruded from a hole bored in the door. Few families had the means to maintain their numerous children; many of the kids were boarded out with relatives or friends.

At St Peter's School, Johnny was better than most at games and bright at his lessons, which on occasion would be inter-rupted by the intrusion of his father, back from the sea. With apologies to the teacher, Callow Senior would march Johnny out of the classroom down to the nearest fish-and-chips shop, there to buy enough 'tuppenies' (which stood for fish) and 'pennies' (for chips) for the whole family. Then off they marched back to the house, which was decorated and hung with notices 'Welcome home'. There they feasted and celebrated the sailor's return.

Johnny left school at fourteen, to earn his own living and con-tribute a few shillings to the family kitty. His first job was at the local glassworks; on Saturdays he played football for the Rose Athletic Club. Some months later, he went to work in the

Woolwich Borough Council, and switched his loyalty to the Foots Cray football XI. Then a broken collar-bone put him out of the game for some time. His Saturdays were blank and dull until his friend Jim Cassidy took him along to Eltham Drill Hall, let out over week-ends for dancing. As Johnny watched the professional couples he was captivated by their grace, and the rhythm of the music. Here was a new kind of sport in which broken collar-bones — his was still hurting like the devil — were the exception. It was that evening that Johnny decided to become a professional ballroom dancer in his spare time. His girl-friend Kathleen, now in her early teens, was thrilled when Johnny asked her to partner him. At his dance salon in Bond Street, Victor Sylvester, the famous dance-band leader, put them through their paces until they reached competition level. Perfect partners on the dance floor and deeply in love, they decided to become partners for life; in 1934 they married.

Johnny worked on at the council offices, but at week-ends the young couple took the floor in competitions all over the country. Rapidly they made a reputation for themselves, though at Cheltenham in 1936 disaster nearly overtook them. Johnny had forgotten his evening trousers; he was lent a pair, so ample round the waist that the slack had to be gathered up and tied with string. Despite the handicap, he and Kathleen danced to the music of Joe Loss and his band, into third place.

With Johnny in his own trousers, they won the national championships. Foxtrot, quick-step, tango and waltz — they loved them all, but since they were a romantic young couple the waltz, more than any other measure, made their own and the spectators' hearts beat fastest. Reaching international level, they took fourth place, in 1937, at the World Championships in Blackpool.

A year later, after Austria and Munich, Johnny and his friends, like everyone else, talked much of a coming war. All of Johnny's old gang joined up. His two brothers also joined: Bert ('Silent Jack', as they nicknamed him) enlisted in the RAF Balloon Command, while Alf, too young for the Services, joined the Home Guard.

Johnny and Kathleen danced their last World Championship in May 1939, a month or so after Czechoslovakia was heeled under by the Nazi jack-boot. Then Johnny discarded his white tie and tails for the heavy blue serge and helmet of a fireman; he joined the Auxiliary Fire Service. His day's work in the office over, he reported at the Eltham sub-station for training.

Kathleen, an accomplished seamstress, applied for a job at the Arsenal; she was put on to sewing up bags of cordite destined for the shells of the big guns — a daily stint of twelve hours in the 'Danger Buildings'.

Ray, the youngest brother, had meanwhile been growing up. Seventeen years separated him from his oldest brother Johnny. Though Johnny was a Catholic and his mother's favourite, Ray, like his father, was a Protestant and his father's favourite. Yet Johnny and Ray were firm friends, Johnny encouraging his small brother to be kind with others, yet hard on himself, honest in all his dealings and, within his modest limits, a sportsman and adventurer. Many an evening they would race each other dozens of circuits round the block; it was fun, and kept them fit. When Ray, diminutive but solid of build, took the field for Plumstead Imperials, the sleeves of his borrowed shirt were rolled up and further up again until his forearms at last protruded; his shorts (borrowed too) came down to his knees, and the football itself came nearly up to them. Ray, like all of his gang, loved cricket too; their pitch was in Saint Helen's street, the lamp-post outside Ray's home serving as a wicket.

Ray joined the gang when he was five — their youngest member. They were a dozen or so little street urchins. The streets were their world and their playground, and they knew every bump and crevice and corner by heart. Old man Callow allowed Ray to stay out till midnight, knowing he could trust his boy not to get up to mischief. Ray's gang, as Johnny's had been, was a band of young brothers united in sport and daring; in good works too.

Today, fifty years later, if you care to look for them, you may find near the Arsenal station, notched in the brick wall by Ray and his gang, the footholds which enabled them to vault up to the top. One after another, the boys took a run, one, two and up. Ray, being so small, could always be sure of a hand-up from the boy before him.

This was one of the gang's meeting-places — the White Roofs, they called it; the other was the Green, a tiny patch of grass near the signal box some way down the line, and to which honour obliged that they should walk along the top of the wall, a seven-foot drop on the street side, a precipice of thirty feet on the Arsenal side. Whenever an Army draft left for overseas the soldiers marched down to the Arsenal station, brass band playing and drummers in tiger-skin aprons beating out the measure and twiddling their drumsticks, with Ray and his gang and all the others trailing along behind. Arrived at the station, the soldiers settled down on the platform, lolling on their palliasses for the long wait before the train's departure. The gang leaped one by one to the top of the wall. 'Anyone want a beer?' they would call down to the soldiers. Having taken their orders, the boys slipped down again into the street to make the round of residents and shopkeepers, collecting pennies. Londoners are always ready to give in a good cause; with their pennies the gang bought the needed beer. Then up again on top of the wall, they lowered the bottles, on the end of a length of string, down to the thirsty soldiers on the platform below.

Ray, the youngest of the gang, was the poorest too. There was always the problem of raising funds, a few pennies for himself, the rest for his family. He had two systems going: from the 'squareheads' in the market he collected empty wooden crates. Ray would tow them, stacked up, on the end of a string round the streets and sell them as firewood. Like this, he collected several pennies.

The other system (just as simple but requiring a little more patience) was to follow, bucket and shovel in hand, a horse-drawn cart. Sooner or later he was sure to gather a harvest of fresh dung, for which he always found a ready market. He took the pennies home as usual to his mother.

Ray's good mother, whose first concern was to feed and maintain her large family, appointed Ray as the family shopper.

With his sense of economy, he was naturally gifted for the job. He would memorize the items needed, and having rattled them off to the shopkeeper would invariably add (as his mother had told him): 'And me dad's out of work . . .' This would often bring him an extra titbit.

Ray started school, like his brother Johnny, at St Peter's. Then one day in the middle of lessons his father, once again back from the sea, made one of his unexpected entries. With apologies as usual to the teacher, he took Ray gently by the scruff of the neck and marched him off, not to the local fish-and-chips shop but to the Burrage Grove School, a Protestant establishment close to home. As in other schools, the little ones were confined to the ground floor, the middling ones to the second and the seniors to the top floor. Now Ray could play cricket in the playground. In summertime the boys paid in a penny a week to save up for a day's outing to Margate. Ray, never having any pennies to spare, would hang around the charabanc, hoping, when the great day came. There was hardly an occasion when once all the fare-paying boys were on board the teacher would not call to Ray, 'All right, Callow, jump in' and Ray would wriggle into some narrow corner.

After Munich, to keep up with his brothers who were enlisting in the Services, Ray joined the Boy Scouts — with at first only enough money to buy the woggle which held the green scarf (yet to be acquired) in place. Thanks to his assiduous 'fund-raising' with matchwood and manure, he was soon able to buy the scarf itself. More weeks of saving and he bought the Scout's jumper. Now he was prepared, like a good Scout, for anything. Little did he imagine what that would amount to.

Ray dreamed of flying. He began by carving his favourite areoplanes out of balsa-wood. Then with his savings he bought kits of Furies, Gladiators, Hurricanes and Spitfires. His father, impressed by his boy's gift for handicrafts, sometimes brought his friends round to admire Ray's work — pretty sure, as Ray was too, that the visitor would press a sixpenny bit into the lad's hand before leaving.

After Munich, kits of German aircraft appeared in the shops.

Dorniers, Heinkels, Junkers and Messerschmitts. Ray was glad to have them for his model air fleet; at the same time he got the feeling that this commerce in German aircraft meant that things were warming up. There were other signs too: gangs of Irish workmen were busy digging trenches on Woolwich and Plumstead commons and bunks were being fitted up inside the Woolwich Equitable Insurance building.

In the months following Munich, on to the Czechoslovakian tragedy of March 1939 and beyond, civil defence wardens were more and more seen in the streets, with their blue uniforms and their white tin hats emblazoned with the initials ARP — Air Raid Precautions.

Air-raid drills and exercises provided good sport to Ray and the gang. Only too happy to volunteer as 'victims', they lay prostrate in the streets, feigning death or injury. After first aid and bandages an ambulance would cart them off to hospital, where after smiles and thanks all round each boy was rewarded with a few sweets. It was fun for all, fun which would give way before long to dreadful reality.

Dark clouds were gathering. After Czechoslovakia people began to brace themselves against the threatening storm. In the Callow family, Amy, the oldest daughter, got a job in the Arsenal, sewing parachutes. Rose, her sister, whose man was in the Merchant Navy, continued to mind her home and her children. Melve, who worked in a denture factory, kept on with her job, an essential one after all; and Renée, still in her teens, found a place as usherette in the Granada cinema — a useful job, she reckoned, for if war came she could help in an emergency.

Finally, there was the old man. He signed off from the Merchant Navy and joined up in the big-gun shop at the Arsenal. There only the strongest men could survive the fierce heat of the foundry and the 12-hour work day. Henry Callow, during his early days as a naval stoker, had acquired the muscles and the guts for the job.

Thus did the Callow family, like thousands of others in London's boroughs north and south of the Thames and in cities throughout the land, prepare for the war which they were sure would hit them in their hearts and their homes. They were to be the mainstay of Britain's night defences.

4

PREPARING FOR WAR

With Britain redoubling her efforts to defend herself against air attack, Hawker Hurricanes and Supermarine Spitfires, '300 mph plus' eight-gun fighters came streaming off the production lines. In 43 Squadron we collected, in December 1938, our first 'Hurries' from Brooklands airfield, surrounded by the famous racing-car circuit. By the time that Hitler had crushed Czechoslovakia in March 1939 the Squadron was operational both by day and by night.

Yes, night-flying was now on the menu of every day-fighter squadron. No one had yet heard of a night-fighter squadron, or of a night-fighter aircraft, because no such thing existed. So we had to swallow our words about fools and owls, and in our day-fighters explore the terrors of the night.

The Hurricane was reported to be manœuvrable and docile. Manœuvrable it certainly was, but in war trim, with ammunition, tanks full, radio fitted and daubed in camouflage 'war-paint', it was not all that docile. It did not forgive errors in flying, particularly near the stall. It possessed no means of 'trimming out', on the rudder, the powerful torque of its 1000 hp Rolls-Royce Merlin engine. Consequently, in cloud and darkness, when flying on instruments − which included an artificial horizon and sensitive altimeter − you nevertheless had the disconcerting impression of pushing with one foot harder than with the other on one end of the rudder-bar, with the uncomfortable feeling that the aircraft was slithering sideways. In its early career the Hurricane killed dozens of pilots and earned a bad name for itself.

Another disturbing feature at night of this formidable day-fighter was the torrent of flame which poured out of the three exhaust ports on each side of the slim pointed nose that housed the V.12 Merlin engine — blue 'Bunsen' flame, the sign of perfect combustion. The Hurricane had not been designed specifically as a night-fighter: no one, apparently, had realized that the exhaust flames would half-blind the pilot, and obscure his precious view of the horizon. The problem was temporarily solved by screening the flames from his view by a narrow, horizontal strip of metal. But they still remained visible to an enemy bomber some hundreds of yards away.

Yet another problem with the early Merlins was 'surging'. Without warning the blue flames would fade to a feeble yellow, with an alarming decrease of power and a corresponding increase in the pilot's pulse-rate; then the blue flames, to the pilot's relief, would reappear.

We played at pretending to be enemy night-bombers for the benefit of the searchlight batteries. Not for ours, though; their dazzling silver-blue beams, flooding the cockpit, could so confuse the pilot that he could barely read his blind-flying instruments.

Searchlights, manned though they were by devoted crews, would always be the bane of the night-fighter, for they too often fixed mistakenly on him, refusing to relax their hold.

A more agreeable exercise was the night sector 'recco', or reconnaissance. Given reasonable weather the lights of Chichester, Horsham and Brighton glittered reassuringly below, each town recognizable by its particular lighting pattern. The dim lights of villages, hamlets, farms and baronial manors would wink at us too, reassuring us that, in all our loneliness, we were not entirely cut off from the world.

Our radio-telephony provided a more tenuous though no less precious contact. We were almost helpless without the controller's guidance. He would call: 'Transmit for fix' and we would reply into the combined microphone and oxygen mask: 'One, two, three, four, five; five, four, three, two, one.' Before long the pilot's voice-transmission for a fix was to be superseded by a cunning little box mounted in the aircraft, the 'Pip-squeak' or IFF (Identification, Friend or Foe) which automatically transmitted a radio signal. Down below was one of those radio devices (quite simple at this stage) called the Chandler-Adcock homing system, by which our position was duly 'fixed'. Then a cheery call from the controller like: 'Vector [steer] 245 and you'll be over base in twelve minutes.' The controller guided us everywhere, out to intercept the enemy (so far imaginary) and back to land. The system seldom failed; when it did it was more often than not a defect in the aircraft's electrical circuit. You headed contentedly for home, and given reasonable weather picked up the 'flashing beacon', a red light parked for the night at a prearranged distance and bearing from the base. It flashed, in Morse, two letters which differed from night to night. The sight of it was always a relief; you were home. But I always told myself 'You may be home, but you've still got to get down.'

The old buckets of burning, smoking kerosene which in Singapore had marked the landing flare-path had now been replaced by 'goose-neck' flares: little cans filled with kerosene, with a spout out of which flared a small flame — theoretically invisible to the enemy and of course to us above 1000 feet altitude. At the touch-down end of the flare-path stood a mobile floodlight, ironically named, after its manufacturers, the Chance light. Beside it the airfield control officer listened on the radio and watched for the aircraft's wing-tip lights. 'Switch on,' he would order the floodlight crew, and out of the darkness, into the glaring beam, glided the aircraft, like a moth into the glow of an electric lamp, and touch-down. Then the floodlight was extinguished and once again all was darkness, save for the flickering goose-neck flares.

If those last few moments of a night patrol, the approach and landing, were what you were most longing for, they were also moments which demanded all your concentration and judg-

31

ment: line up on the flare-path, then let down at the correct angle and speed — not like poor Charles who got it all wrong, flew into a tall oak-tree and died. There were others too, alas, who did not survive those last moments.

Navigational aids had certainly improved since those nights in Singapore. You could get off safely, be vectored anywhere within R/T range; then home back to base and land without undue hazard, given reasonable visibility. We were still living and flying in the last few months of peace, and were not expected to go out of our way to risk our lives on account of bad weather. Most nights the earth below and the heavens above still shone with a million lights.

Yet even when favoured by the weather, the problem of intercepting a night raider was still far from being solved. The crews of the two weapons — anti-aircraft guns and fighters — capable of downing an unseen raider concealed by cloud or darkness, needed to know, in all the hundreds of cubic miles of space in the sky above, the position, within yards, of their target. Searchlights, 'aimed' (like the guns) by obsolete sound-locators, could help but little. Silvery blue shafts of light in the dark, they rarely picked up the target. Only radar, as an integral part of the aiming system, could pin-point the invisible enemy.

The fighter-pilot in the dark was even worse off; he had to fly in close enough to the 'hostile' in order to discern, with his own eyes, its dark, indefinite shape. Searchlights, if only they could illuminate it, could help. But the radical solution was to fit in the fighter aircraft itself a radar set which could guide the pilot close enough to sight the stealthy enemy.

In Britain such electronic marvels were still only being dreamed up. The problem was to condense the tons of steel masts and aerials of the coastal radar stations into a small box. The RAF had as yet no concrete plans for a specialized night-fighter force.

Three months after Munich, in December 1938, fourteen coastal radar stations were on watch; six more were still in the building. These 'Chain Home' stations, with their 100-metre-high steel lattice masts, were rooted, immobile, where they stood. From their fixed — and extremely vulnerable — position they could look out across the sea over an arc of 120 degrees; they could detect an aircraft at well over a hundred miles from the coast, read its height (if not too low) and its direction. Inland, however, they were blind; they could see nothing of an aircraft once it crossed the coast.

To the Observer (later Royal Observer) Corps fell the task of plotting aircraft flying overland. Observer Corps posts covered the country; using their eyes, their ears and a field telephone, they were at the time a vital link in the aircraft detection system.

Yet as late as summer 1939 Winston Churchill compared the coastal radar cover and the Observer Corps as a 'transition from the mid-twentieth century to the Stone Age'. He insisted on the urgent need for inland radar cover; yet this 'Ground Controlled Interception' (GCI) was, like radar for guns, searchlights and fighters, still in the embryonic stage. The men of the Observer Corps were to keep faithful watch, in all weathers, for many a long day and night.

Without knowing much about each other's progress in radar, the British and the Germans had been working on almost parallel lines, but the Germans were ahead, all the same, in technology. At the time of Munich they possessed an excellent long-range radar, the Freya. Though it could not tell height, it could detect at a range of 75 miles and through a complete circle of 360 degrees. And it was mobile — a boon, the Germans would find, when they came to command the European coastline from Norway to the Pyrenees.

But — and it would prove decisive when the hour of battle struck — the British, whose first thought was the defence of their island, had linked their coastal radar sentinels by telephone and radio-telephone with their defending fighters. The Germans, bent only on aggression and a 'lightning war', had done nothing of the kind. British long-range radar, if less refined than German, had been incorporated in a formidable system of air defence.

In short-range radar the Germans had a clear lead over Britain with the Würzburg, a small, entirely mobile apparatus which could detect with remarkable accuracy at a distance of 25 miles. As such, it was an ideal 'seeing aid' for anti-aircraft guns and searchlights. Göring, though professing a distaste for radio devices — 'boxes with coils, and I don't like them', he once grumbled — was all the same so enthusiastic about Würzburg that he rashly boasted, 'If a single enemy bomber crosses our frontier, you can call me Meier.' At the same time, the Reichs-marschall was equally impressed with the Luftwaffe's first work-ing model of an airborne radar set. If only the British had possessed such radar devices, so that their guns, their search-lights and fighters could strike at the Luftwaffe bombers in the dark! The British needed them urgently. The Germans, who already had them, would not require to use them till later.

Throughout 1939 the British pressed on with the completion of their coastal radar chain. Those lofty masts could not possibly escape the notice of curious eyes, including those of the Germans. The masts were evidently part of a radio system, and the Germans, intrigued, decided to investigate them closely. Their huge and stately airship *Graf Zeppelin*, with eleven years' commercial flying to its credit, was now fitted out with the latest in electronic detection gear. With the chief of the Luftwaffe signals section, General Wolfgang Martini, aboard the airship cruised at a leisurely pace up the east coast of England, its tech-nicians (including Martini) quite ignorant that they were being followed every inch of the way by those very radar stations whose secrets they had come to discover. The Zeppelin's 'plots' were recorded on the operations map at Fighter Command, who watched its progress in silence, even when the great airship transmitted to base its position — wrongly calculated. It may have been a trap, but the controller at Fighter Command, though sorely tempted to transmit the correct position, wisely refrained. Throughout the *Graf Zeppelin*'s voyage nothing but a horrible crackling assailed the ears of General Martini and his radio detectives. They returned to the Fatherland without a single clue to enlighten them about British radar.

At midnight on 2 August, exactly a month before Britain and Germany were at war, the *Graf Zeppelin* slipped off again into the dark for another try. Not only was it unsuccessful but the airship was indiscreet enough to reveal itself to coastguards in Aberdeenshire, as well as to the astonished eyes of two British fighter pilots sent up to intercept it. Once again *Graf Zeppelin* returned empty-handed.

The 'Wizard War', as Churchill called it, was already fully engaged — an occult and secret war, with only a handful of men on each side who knew what was going on. An even smaller number, with the instincts of Sherlock Holmes or James Bond, were working diligently but in obscurity, trying, with the help of odd and occasional clues, to penetrate the secrets of the other side.

The Wizard War was waged in stealth and silence, on fronts other than radar. For some years the German Wehrmacht, the Kriegsmarine, the Luftwaffe and the sinister Schutzstaffel (SS) had been exchanging radio messages in high-grade cipher by means of an automatic enciphering machine called 'Enigma'. In 1928 the British Government Code and Cypher School (codenamed 'Station X') at Bletchley, 50 miles north of London, managed to 'acquire' two German-made enciphering machines identical to Enigma. The British copied and improved them. The modified version was called the 'RAF Enigma', and later 'Typex'. The Typex cipher remained unbroken during the war. Not so the original German Enigma. The Germans possessed no such band of dedicated geniuses as the cryptographers of Station X. They believed that their own Enigma cipher was unbreakable. But the British cryptographers, despite tantalizing problems, succeeded finally in elucidating the secrets of Enigma.

First, however, the RAF Wireless Intelligence Service (the 'Y-Service'), whose monitoring stations were ceaselessly eavesdropping on all German radio traffic, had to record what they had heard. Low-grade cipher and plain-language messages were no problem, but the high-grade cipher of Enigma was confined to specialists at the listening station at Chicksands in Bedfordshire. Once received, Enigma signals were sent on to Station X, whose wizards broke down the highly secret cipher messages — a mass of information emanating from the German armed forces, and not least the Luftwaffe (who were the least discreet of all), concerning their future plans and a whole lot more.

Station X then passed on this information, under the name of 'Ultra-intelligence', to a small circle including the prime minister and a few top ministers and service commanders.

During those summer months of 1939 we exercised in our Hurricanes, day and night, for war. Towards midnight on 24 August I took off on a night reconnaissance, glad as usual to see the dark earth below carpeted with the lights of inland and seaside towns. My next flight would be in the bewildering obscurity of the nation-wide blackout. Meanwhile we flew little, nursing our Hurricanes and waiting, alert, for the inevitable.

It came on 1 September, when Hitler's armies, with the Luftwaffe in close support, blasted their way into valiant, helpless Poland. This time the allies, France and Britain, acted. On 3 September they declared war against Germany. Lying on the grass beside our Hurricanes, we waited, chatting quietly among ourselves, for the Luftwaffe bombers to darken our fair skies as Göring had promised, and deliver the knock-out blow on London. It was not to come for another year — and then many of us would no longer be around.

5

BOFFINS AND OTHERS

During the next ten months until July 1940, when the day battle over our coasts and countryside and towns began in earnest, the Luftwaffe did not molest Britain with anything like the violence expected. In May and June it had been concentrating its gigantic strength in helping the Wehrmacht to reduce our allies in Europe, Norway, Denmark, Holland, Belgium, Luxembourg and France, to vassal states.

The Luftwaffe's role was essentially a tactical one, to support the army in the field. Hitler had promised the German people that Christmas 1939 would be the last Christmas of the war; he had no wish to get involved in a long-term conflict which would require his bombers to make raids on distant strategic targets: ports, industrial cities and eventually residential areas. He made it clear that he alone would decide if and when the moment should ever come to attack strategic targets in Britain.

The possibility of such bombing operations, however, was by no means excluded. Their success would depend on very accurate navigation. The traditional method of long-distance air navigation, 'dead reckoning', was a cumbersome exercise, with its paraphernalia of maps and a table to spread them on, a magnetic compass and dividers, set-square and ruler to plot the aircraft's position. It was better suited to the bridge of a naval vessel. With data such as airspeed, 'drift' (caused by the wind), a visual fix on some prominent object or an occasional radio fix from a radio direction-finding (D/F) station, the navigator calculated the correct course to fly. This he passed on to the pilot, who adjusted his compass accordingly.

Dead reckoning was an artisanal craft; its only advantage was its immunity from radio interference, 'jamming'. But in darkness or in cloud it was seriously wanting in the acute precision required for 'blind' bombing.

Since 1933, when Hitler came to power and the 'black' (secret) Luftwaffe was born, the Germans had already begun to experiment with more sophisticated methods of long-range navigation, inspired by their famous Lorenz system of blind approach and landing, which was used not only by themselves but by many airlines and air forces, including the RAF. Highly ingenious it was, yet simple for the pilot. A radio beam, like an invisible tramline, led him down to the landing path. In his earphones he heard, when firmly on the 'tramline', a steady note. If he deviated to the right he heard Morse dashes, if to the left dots. The tramline, with its steady note, was always there between the dots and dashes.

Early in 1939, British scientists — boffins, as they were affectionately known — of the Committee of Scientific Study of Air Defence came to the regrettable but timely conclusion that if much was suspected, little was known in Britain about German navigational methods. It was wisely decided to let loose a boffin among the non-scientific experts of the Directorate of Air Ministry Intelligence. The man chosen was Dr R. V. Jones, a genial young giant of a man and brilliant physicist from Oxford University. He took up his job soon after the outbreak of war; a couple of months later he had already obtained clues, as astonishing as they were unexpected, concerning the Luftwaffe's radio-beam system of navigation.

On 4 November 1939 an odd-looking parcel addressed to the Naval Attaché was delivered to the British Embassy in Oslo. It contained many pages of text, written in German, referring to a number of German secret weapons. The anonymous sender signed himself 'From a well-wishing German scientist'. It was not long before Dr Jones, in his office in London, was studying the English version, amazed by the revelations of what became known as the 'Oslo Report'.

Among many other subjects, it mentioned an important research station at Peenemünde, a small island in the Baltic Sea; it described the development there of a flying bomb (propelled by a ram-jet, a crude form of jet propulsion) and of a supersonic rocket, both to become only too familiar to the British more than four years later respectively as the V.1 and V.2.

Another passage, which particularly intrigued Dr Jones, explained the details of a new radio-beam device intended to guide long-range bombers. It was able to measure the exact distance of a bomber, flying along a beam fixed on the enemy target, from the transmitting station which in turn had only to tell the bomber pilot the exact moment to release his bombs. The system was a sensational advance on navigation by dead reckoning.

The British were wary of the Oslo Report; it could be a 'plant'. But Dr Jones was convinced that, at least in his particular field of German radio beams, the evidence was perfectly trustworthy.

At Tangmere we kept waiting for the knock-out blow, basking in the September sun on the grass beside our Hurricanes, sleeping by night in some discomfort in the pilots' room beside the tarmac. At any second we were ready to go, but for all Göring's bombast, Hitler's main wish was to avoid a general war — above all with the British, for whom, although they were later to infuriate him, he felt a positive admiration. A love-hate affair.

The days passed slowly with little doing but routine flights and an occasional false alarm. Night flights were more of a problem. The black-out deprived us of that friendly carpet of lights below us which told us where we were, and which way up. We could rivet our eyes, it is true, on the artificial horizon in the middle of the dashboard, but that soulless little robot was no substitute for the real horizon separating earth from sky.

One night, lined up on the flare-path for take-off, I thanked God for the rising moon, wanly shining out of a blank wall of darkness. So peaceful and lovely it looked above, and reassuring too. A few moments after take-off, as I turned left it reappeared below my right wing, giving the disconcerting impression that I was nearly upside down. Thus ended abruptly that brief, magic vision of the moon; my eyes darted back to the dashboard and its unromantic artificial horizon.

Another night, on a lone reconnaissance beyond the sector boundary, I flew down moonlit canyons formed by massifs of dark cloud towering heavenward and sometimes obscuring the stars. It was all too easy to feel overawed by these gigantic, eerie mountains which isolated me from the friendly earth. It needed a conscious mental effort to persuade myself that my aeroplane and I were one, that I was both its brain and its sinews, that it must function according to my will. Lost above all that mass of cloud, I called the controller for a fix. It was David Lloyd that night. As he gave me my position I detected some concern in his voice, as in his efforts to reassure me he added, 'We'll get you down soon; we've put the kettle on for tea.'

Between cup and lip there's many a slip. David had no exact information on the margin of clear air between cloud-base and earth, except that the 650-feet-high Downs to the north of Tangmere were in cloud. But he did the right thing, talking me down until I broke cloud not over land but a hundred yards above a dark waste of sea. I knew I was safe so far. Steer north by compass and hit the coast. David confirmed my course, telling me, 'You will see the flashing beacon and we've had the floodlight switched on.' Five minutes later I touched down. Though the air was our playground, and before long would be our field of battle too, it was always a relief to feel the good earth beneath our feet. A few moments more and I was drinking the promised cup of tea with David in the ops-room. Though we did not say so, we felt grateful to one another. Between us we had succeeded in a rather hazardous landing.

Compared with the Lorenz blind-approach system, fitted in all German bombers and most of our own, the 'fighter-boy' method was crude and archaic. Yet there was something far more human in David's voice and his promise of a 'cupper' than in the irritating dots and dashes of the Lorenz system.

In November 43 Squadron moved to Acklington, a grass field north of Newcastle. When the wind was in the south the smoke which the industries of this great city poured into the air did not make for good visibility. As day-fighters our job was to protect in all weathers the coast-bound convoys. With raging seas and gloomy skies, it was harder for the sailors down below than for us in our snug (though unheated) cockpits.

When darkness fell we left the convoys — now in relative safety — to perform our secondary role of night-flying. 'Hideous obscurity,' I wrote in my log-book after one patrol. After another, intended for test-firing my guns (a spectacular firework display), the searchlights, uninvited, held me in a blinding flood of light. 'Unable to turn for five minutes. Those BLOODY searchlights . . .' I commented this time in my log-book. Clearly the searchlights needed help to tell friend from foe. Somebody may have tipped them off, for a week later I flew undisturbed in the dark for an hour, and wrote in my log-book, 'No death-rays got me tonight.'

Foul weather, apart from the artificial kind created by smoke, added to the excitement. During January 1940 heavy falls of snow blanketed the airfield and the surrounding country. Flying through a snow-storm was like flying through heavy gunfire, only the 'tracer' was not red but white and there was more of it. Landing on snow was tricky — like flying low above the glassy sea around Singapore. The glazed surface made it difficult to judge height. Happily, though, the snow, with its dangers, repaid us in full by the startling beauty of its white mantle cast upon the earth and glistening under the kindly light of the moon.

One night in February 1940, while on patrol, confused voices jammed my R/T. From the hubbub I gathered that John Simpson, one of the more skilful pilots in my flight, had crashed on take-off. I sped back to the airfield, landed and taxied to the end of the flare-path where fire-engines and floodlights were already on the scene. A Hurricane had indeed crashed, scything its way for more than fifty yards through a spinney of young fir-trees before coming to rest. An ambulance had already carried John, shaken but unhurt, off to hospital. That blessed Hurricane —

apparently the engine had failed — lay there among the fallen trees, still in one piece. So robust was it that were it fir-trees or enemy fire, it could take the most brutal punishment.

My impromptu landing was fortuitous, for I badly needed to relieve myself — an untidy operation when forced upon you in the cramped cockpit of a Hurricane. After inspecting John's crash, I taxied hurriedly to a discreetly dark corner of the airfield, and, without stopping the engine, hopped out of the cockpit on to the left wing and down to the ground. The necessary done, back I climbed on to the wing and into the cockpit, strapped myself in, parachute harness first, then the Sutton harness which held you in. A few moments later I was soaring away once more into the darkness. Night-flying, for all its dangers, was not without its homely side.

On the morning of 3 February, leading Blue section (Flying Officer 'Tiger' Folkes and Sergeant Jim Hallowes), I fought my first combat. The shattering burst of fire from my guns disabled the Heinkel 111, which crash-landed in the snow, inland of Whitby, Yorks. A Heinkel of Kampfgeschwader 26, the 'Lion' Geschwader. Next day I travelled to the bedside of one of the two survivors, Unteroffizier Karl Missy. I felt sorry for him, having wounded him so grievously that he was now without a leg. His pilot, Wilms, was unhurt; the two others of the crew were buried next day with a wreath from 43 Squadron.

At the end of February the squadron moved to wilder climes on the rugged coast of the north-east tip of Scotland, at Wick. It was there, way out over the sea, that I fought my first night combat — the interception itself was far from a classic affair, to say the least.

In that particular sector the radar was notoriously unreliable; its vagaries could make you laugh. One day while on a 'calibration test' and cruising at a steady 200 mph, the genial controller Mac, a first-war pilot, called me up: 'It may interest you to know', he chuckled, 'that according to our radar plots you are cruising at 900 mph!'

No wonder then that just after nightfall on 8 April I failed to intercept a raid of several bombers heading for the great naval base of Scapa Flow in the Orkneys, just opposite. Jim Hallowes was with me in open formation. This was a time before fighters were dispatched individually at night. Craning our necks, we searched the sky, now pale blue in the fading light. In vain. 'You must see them!' Mac called impatiently. 'Your plots and theirs are identical.' But the sky above was empty. A moment later, over Scapa, it suddenly became alive with bursting anti-aircraft shells. So that was where the bombers were! But how to engage them in the midst of that gigantic firework display, with lead flying in all directions? I called Hallowes, 'You're on your own; do what you can' and edged towards the barrage, hoping to pick out a bomber. All I got for my pains was a near-miss from the AA, which I discovered on landing had smashed my tail-light and damaged the rudder.

A thought occurred to me. Some weeks before, while chatting with the landlord of a pub in John O'Groats, this worthy had told me how on a previous raid some of the enemy bombers had flown out low over his pub on their way home. So down I went in a steep dive and circled the little town, but spied no bombers — only a few bombs plopping into the waters of the Pentland Firth. Again I looked up searching, and there, high above, were two Heinkels, unmistakable by their wing shape silhouetted against the luminous sky, hurrying home.

The chase was on. Climbing at full throttle, my eyes glued on those fleeing shapes. I began to close on them. Then came the faint voice of Mac in my earphones: 'Blue leader, return to base and land.' With a passing thought for Admiral Nelson,* I switched off my radio. I was now gaining fast, and could clearly make out the dark shape of the hindmost of the two Heinkels. Closing the range still further, I opened fire. Immediately the bomber's undercarriage dropped down, a phenomenon common to Heinkels when badly hit. Streaming oil and vapour from its engines, the bomber was going down, but its rear gunner, seeing me silhouetted against the after-glow in the north-west, was

*At the Battle of Copenhagen (1801) when signalled by flag to withdraw, Nelson put his telescope to his blind eye and said: 'I see no such signal'.

still putting up a desperate fight. I went in again, guns blazing, flying down his cone of tracers until as I dodged below I could hear his MG15 machine-gun still firing just above my head. He was a brave man fighting for his life, as I was for mine; two young gladiators between whom there was no real enmity. It was a pity that one of them — and his comrades — had to die.

As the Heinkel glided down towards the sea its navigation lights came on. I followed it until I could faintly discern the white furrow it ploughed in the sea as it ditched. Then its lights disappeared.

Back at base I found that my Hurricane had been riddled with the bullets of that brave air-gunner. Was this yet again an aircraft of KG26? I do not know. It left no trace for the British to investigate.

During the previous month, March, another Heinkel 111 of KG26 had been brought down on English soil. In the wreckage was found a scrap of crumpled paper with a few words written on it: 'Beacon Plan A . . . Knickebein from 0600 hours on 315°.' What could Knickebein mean, other than literally 'crooked leg'? Here was a clue for Dr Jones to solve.

Soon afterwards a Luftwaffe prisoner of war provided another vague clue. Knickebein, he told the RAF interrogator, was 'something like the X-Gerät' (X-equipment), mounted in some aircraft to receive signals from X-Verfahren (X-System), a very narrow radio beam which could reach London. He thought that the British knew about X-Gerät. He thought wrong; the British knew nothing about this top-secret device, which was all the more surprising because ten members, including the commanding officer and Technical Officer of the only Luftwaffe unit, Kampfgruppe 100, trained to use it, were in British prisoner-of-war camps. They had been captured during the Norwegian campaign the month before, and wisely kept their mouths shut — unlike their compatriot, who had let a fair-sized cat out of the bag, though it would take the British some months to run it down.

In May another of KG26's Heinkels was brought down on dry

land. Intelligence experts, sifting through the wreckage, happened upon a diary belonging to one of the crew. An entry for 5 March recorded 'In the afternoon, we studied Knickebein . . .'

With these clues in hand, Dr Jones deduced that Knickebein and X-Gerät must be directional beams which could be used for navigation and blind bombing. Another thing: they seemed to be used exclusively by Heinkels. Dr Jones recalled an earlier incident, the first Heinkel down in Great Britain: it crashed near Edinburgh. The intelligence men in their minute examination of the aircraft had been struck by its Lorenz blind-approach equipment; it was much more effective than the Lorenz apparatus used by the RAF. Had the Luftwaffe adapted it to receive long-range radio beams? That is what Dr Jones had yet to prove.

It was on 10 May 1940, just over a fortnight before the evacuation began of nearly 340,000 harassed British and French troops from Dunkirk, in northern France, that Winston Churchill succeeded Neville Chamberlain as prime minister, thus reaching the summit of a turbulent political career which had begun forty years earlier. His first ministerial post, in 1906, was that of colonial under-secretary. In that year Adolf Hitler, who had been 'ploughed' (like Churchill a decade earlier) in his exams, had just left school with the dream of becoming an artist. Hermann Göring was then a lusty youngster of thirteen. Five years later, in 1911, when Churchill assumed the prestigious post of First Lord of the Admiralty (the British Navy was then the mightiest in the world), Hitler, having twice failed the entrance exam to the Vienna Academy of Fine Arts, was earning a meagre living painting picture postcards. Göring was still in his teens. These were the men who, on the British side and the German, were to oppose each other in the battle for survival thirty years later.

Churchill, as he admits, knew nothing about science; Hitler and Göring knew less than nothing. But Churchill did know something of scientists, and in his many previous ministerial posts 'had much experience', as he wrote later, 'in handling things I did not understand'. For four years during the thirties,

45

as a member of the Defence Research Committee, he had acquired an outline knowledge of the radar problem.

As scientific adviser Churchill had invited Professor Frederick Lindemann, an able scientist but, more important to Churchill, his friend and confidant of twenty years. The 'Prof' possessed, in Churchill's words, the ability to 'explain in lucid, homely terms what the issues were'. Incidentally, Lindemann, the 'Prof', had been Dr Jones's tutor at Oxford.

Winston Churchill in 1940 was the man of the hour, the man that Britain — very soon to find herself alone in the struggle against Nazi Germany — needed to lead her. Three days after taking office he declared to Parliament 'I have nothing to offer but blood, tears, toil and sweat.' Again, on 22 May, warning Parliament and the nation of the risk of invasion, he uttered these defiant words for all the world to hear: 'We shall go on to the end . . . ; whatever the cost may be we shall fight on the beaches, we shall fight on the landing grounds, we shall fight on the fields and in the streets, we shall fight in the hills; we shall never surrender . . .' The British took Churchill to their heart. They were as determined as he.

The day after that stirring speech I arrived at Debden in Essex to take command of 85 Fighter Squadron. After the fierce fighting in the Battle of France, the Squadron, its bases blasted by the Luftwaffe and overrun by the Wehrmacht, was being pulled out to prepare for the next and final battle of Hitler's sweepingly successful European offensive. The Battle of France was over, said Churchill; the Battle of Britain was about to begin.

So swift had been the German advance in France that 85 had to leave many of its Hurricanes behind. The pilots arrived at Debden by dribs and drabs, some in Hurricanes they had managed to save, some in trainer aircraft, others by train or private car.

There I awaited them with a welcoming smile and not a little apprehension. 85, like 43, was a crack squadron. The Canadian Major Billy Bishop VC had been one of its commanders in the First World War; Major 'Micky' Mannock VC one of its aces.

In the last few weeks in France, the Squadron had fought hard and punished the enemy, downing for certain 89 of their aircraft. It had just lost in the space of a few days two commanding officers — 'Doggy' Oliver, badly wounded, and Michael Peacock, killed. I was third on the list. How would 'the boys' take to their new leader?

In the event we soon became friends. The Squadron had lost a number of pilots, missing, killed or wounded, in France. A dozen new pilots, youths in their 'teens or early twenties, came to replace them. They had but a basic experience of flying, far less of flying the swift and powerful Hurricane. Compared with them I was an old hand, already twenty-five, and with seven years of flying behind me. I had already discovered, and in the coming months was to discover yet again, that experience alone was not enough; luck too played a big part in survival.

In the sky above Debden we, the few older hands, took the new ones under our wing. Incessantly, day after day, we drilled them in the discipline and dodges of air combat. By the end of June the Squadron was operational again. By day our job was to protect, from dawn to dusk, the coast-bound convoys continually menaced by the Luftwaffe.

Night-flying, for the moment, was not for the new boys; their hands would be more than full during the daytime. Only four or five of us were experienced enough to answer the controller's request for a night patrol. It was now that I began to accustom myself not to sleep, except in snatches, at night. I lay, clothed and ready to go, on the rough blanket of my camp bed. Our night patrols were fraught with uncertainty. One night our trusty controller Squadron Leader Reese and I lost touch with one another. Guided here, there and everywhere by him for the last half-hour in the foggy night, I had not the least idea of my position. If my fuel ran out I should have to jump for it — over land or sea, I could not tell. Then, thank God, we were in touch again. Reese apologized that I had been plotted as an enemy aircraft. He brought me home safely in the murk to Duxford, some miles from Debden.

Naturally, the traditional cup of tea was waiting for me. I

could have done with a stiff Scotch, but still had to fly back to Debden. No one ever drank alcohol while on the job.

A few nights later and behold! an enemy aircraft, a Heinkel 111. held by the searchlights. But 'with everything pushed and pulled' (as one said) I was unable to close on him before he eluded the grasp of those long, straight, silver fingers.

Our forward base was Martlesham, an uneven field on the heath not far from Ipswich. At dusk one evening, in pouring rain, the Luftwaffe attacked a convoy not far from the coast before we could intervene. The escorting destroyer, HMS *Wren*, was sunk. It was growing dark as my section was sent off. The most we could do now was to patrol in the rain the desolate scene — pathetic flotsam and jetsam strewn across the oily sea where the brave ship had foundered. With height and visibility fading rapidly, I was called back to Martlesham to land, but there I could see no sign of a flare-path, and flying low over the field I understood why. Rain had half flooded the landing area, which was now generously inundated with small lakes of water. Low in fuel, we had to get down somehow. I came in first with my headlight on, touched down and ran on between the huge puddles. Talking to my Nos. 2 and 3 on the R/T, I told them to be patient. I would station myself just short of the touch-down point, headlight on and aligned to give them a clear run. Then I called them in, and with calm and skill they made the difficult landing.

While we had been performing as occasional night-fighters, with the aid of these primitive and uncertain techniques, Dr Jones had been pondering over the scientific evidence he had been able to gather concerning Knickebein.

With such clues as he possessed, he went to see his onetime tutor, Professor Lindemann. But 'R.V.' failed to convince the 'Prof' that the Luftwaffe could be using radio beams for long-range navigation and blind bombing. However, he was not to be put off. After further work on his theory, he returned to the attack on 13 June. This time he won over the 'Prof', who in a letter to Churchill the same day informed the prime minister that

Above: Masts of a C.H. (Chain Home) radar station. Such stations could detect an aircraft at well over 100 miles from the coast. In fixed positions, they could see nothing of an aircraft once it had crossed the coast. *Imperial War Museum*

Left: G.C.I. (Ground Control Interception) Mobile Station. Designed for inland radar cover. *Imperial War Museum*

Above: Balloons attached by a steel cable to the ground could rise several thousand feet above, forming a defensive barrage against air attack. Here they are being inflated.
Imperial War Museum

Below: Day battle. 85 Squadron climbs to meet the enemy. Hawker Hurricanes in formation. The first British fighter plane to exceed 300 mph, Hurricanes are credited with destroying more German planes than any other aircraft during the Battle of Britain.
Imperial War Museum

Left: Supermarine Spitfire (used mostly for day-fighting). An aircraft noted for its speed and manoeuvrability, it could reach a speed of 375 mph and fly above 33,000 ft. *Imperial War Museum*

Left: Bristol Beaufighter with Mark IV AI (Air Interception) radar. *Imperial War Museum*

Below: Havoc Mk II Turbinlite ('Helmore') – the flying searchlight. Sent to 85 Squadron for trials, it did not prove a success. *Imperial War Museum*

Above: Jim Marshall in the cockpit of a Hurricane. *Imperial War Museum*

Below: 85 Squadron fighter pilots. *Left to right:* Sgt. Webster, Sgt. Goodman, Sgt. Bentley, Squadron Leader Townsend (with top tunic button undone and recovering from a wounded foot), two Polish pilots, Sgt. Gray. In the background a Hurricane with 'kidney type' exhausts. *Imperial War Museum*

bove: Operations Room, Fighter Command Headquarters, Bentley Priory, Stanmore, Middlesex. Above: Controller and assistants. Below: W.A.A.F. plotters. *Imperial War Museum*

Below: 85 Squadron night-fighter pilots relaxing at the dispersal point. (Debden, near Saffron Walden, Essex, 14 March 1941). *Imperial War Museum*

Above: At the dispersal point, wearing dark glasses to acclimatize before going on patrol. *Left to right:* Bill Carnaby, Jim Marshall, Peter Townsend, Geoff Howlitt – with Kim, the Squadron mascot. *Imperial War Museum*

Below: Night patrol just before take-off. The pilot, James Wheeler, settles into the cockpit of his Hurricane VY-X. The hexagon emblem of 85 Squadron is visible. *Imperial War Museum*

HE LUFTWAFFE

me of the aircraft used by the Luftwaffe in attacks on London and provincial British cities, 40-41.

t the outbreak of the Second World War the Luftwaffe had an estimated strength of 500,000 en and 5,000 aircraft, while the RAF had about 100,000 men and 2,000 aircraft.

bove: Heinkel 111 medium bomber taking off. (The Heinkel 111 and JU-88 bombers had omb-load of over 4,000 lbs; the Dornier 17 about half that load.) *Imperial War Museum*

low: Dornier 215 (a variant of the Dornier 17). *Imperial War Museum*

Above: Junkers JU-88 – twin-engined day or night fighter bomber with a top speed of 280 mph. It largely replaced the JU-87, which sustained heavy losses during the Battle of Britain due to its low speed of 210 mph. *Imperial War Museum*

Below: Captured Focke-Wulf 190 in front of the control tower, West Malling, 5 July 1943. *Imperial War Museum*

there was reason to suppose that the Germans possessed some radio device with which to locate and bomb their targets in the dark and in cloud. It was imperative to discover its wave-length. 'If we knew this, we could devise some means to mislead them . . .' wrote Lindemann.

His astonishing revelation came, Churchill admitted, as 'a painful shock'. Until now he had fondly imagined that the fog, mist and cloud of the British climate would provide enough cover to conceal targets from accurate bombing, especially at night.

Churchill lost not a moment. He ordered an immediate investigation, under Air Marshal Joubert; it went to work next day. That very day a Luftwaffe prisoner let yet another big cat out of the bag, telling the RAF interrogation officer that Knickebein was a bombing method using two radio beams which intersected over the target and could be picked up by the bomber's Lorenz equipment.

The picture was becoming clearer. Joubert's investigation team now ordered that three Ansons, ancient but reliable reconnaissance planes, should be filled with special radio equipment to detect the invisible beams. The search began at dusk, on 18 June, but ended in a blank night. However, another clue had been discovered earlier that day from papers salvaged from a Heinkel 111 shot down in France. They revealed some highly relevant information:

Long-range radio beacon: V.H.F. (Very High Frequency)
1. Knickebein (near Bredstedt, north-east of Husum)
2. Knickebein . . . (near Kleve)

Still one more clue came to hand from yet another crashed Heinkel; its wireless operator had scribbled in his log-book. 'Knickebein, Kleve 31.5.' '31.5' was the waveband (in megacycles) that Professor Lindemann so badly needed to know.

On the night of 18 June a second attempt was made by an Anson to detect the beam. Once again it drew a blank; Knickebein was not on the air that night.

Meanwhile a fresh clue, which promised to be vital, was being literally pieced together. In the early hours of 20 June a Luftwaffe wireless operator baled out of his stricken Heinkel bomber over England, his radio log-book in a pocket of his flying-suit. On landing he set to and tore the pages into thousands of pieces. Unfortunately for him, he was caught red-handed in the act of burying them. By 3 a.m. on the 21st RAF intelligence officers had stuck all the little bits together again, and found the vital clue — the exact co-ordinates of the Knickebein transmitters at Stollberg (very close to Bredstedt) and at Kleve.

Later that morning Churchill — 'with anxious mind', as he confessed — presided in the Cabinet Room at No. 10 Downing Street, over a meeting of scientists and air force commanders. When Dr Jones received his summons to attend he thought it was a practical joke. When eventually he arrived, somewhat flustered and several minutes late, Churchill asked him to open the discussion. For some twenty minutes the young scientist un-folded the tale of Knickebein, 'the like of which', Churchill wrote later, 'for its convincing fascination, was never surpassed by tales of Sherlock Holmes or Monsieur Lecoq'. Churchill, ever sensitive to rhyme and the ridiculous, went on: 'As I listened the Ingoldsby Legends jingled in my mind:

> But now one Mr Jones comes forth and depones
> How, fifteen years since, he had heard certain groans
> On his way to Stonehenge (to examine the stones
> Described in a work of the late Sir John Soane's),
> That he followed the moans, and led by their tones
> Found a raven a-picking a drummer-boy's bones!

On this occasion 'Mr Jones' left the assembly of senior scien-tists and airmen both concerned and incredulous. After all, the German airline Lufthansa and the Luftwaffe, like the RAF and Imperial Airways, had been using the well-tried methods of dead-reckoning and astronavigation for years. How was it possible that during all this time, and in complete secrecy, they could have been working on such a revolutionary and successful method of navigation?

Proof of Knickebein's efficacity was forthcoming that very night, when an Avro Anson, Flight Lieutenant Bufton at the controls with Corporal Mackie, a peacetime 'ham' radio enthusiast, as Wireless Op., succeeded in picking up Knickebein. Its direction was roughly East-West, and Bufton and Mackie discovered that it was a beam some 400 to 500 yards wide, having Morse dots to the left and dashes to the right.

This material evidence concerning Knickebein confirmed the worst fears of those present that morning at the meeting in Downing Street. With Knickebein, the target, at night or in bad weather, was no longer concealed from the enemy bombers, as were they themselves from all the ill-equipped British ground defences and defending fighters. So far the Luftwaffe had not yet launched an all-out bomber offensive against Britain. But they were unlikely to tarry much longer now that Hitler was master of most of Europe, and Churchill and the British remained defiant.

Indeed, it was on the afternoon of that meeting at Downing Street that Hitler visited the famous railway carriage at Compiègne, north of Paris, where in 1918 the vanquished Germans had signed the Armistice which put an end to the First World War. Among those present during Hitler's visit was one of the greatest of American correspondents, William Shirer (America would not be at war with Germany until a year and half later). Shirer wrote in his diary of Hitler: 'I have seen that face many times . . . . But today! It is afire with scorn, anger, hate, revenge, triumph.' In a month or so Hitler would be venting his feelings on the only country which still defied him — Britain, now half surrounded by German-occupied territory, from the Arctic Circle in Norway to the French Pyrenees.

6

THE WIZARD WAR

The Wizard War now became — for the British — a race against time. If Britain's day-fighters were heavily outnumbered they, and the elaborate organization behind them, were in great heart. Confident in their superb Hurricanes and Spitfires, backed by radar detection and control by radio from the ground, they would stand firm, however hard the fight, against the enemy's onslaught by day. But at night? Our guns, searchlights and fighters were pitifully lacking in the scientific equipment needed to enable them to come to grips with the enemy under cover of darkness.

To fill — in part — the gaping breach in their night defences the British for the moment possessed but one reliable weapon, which still required development — the 'jamming' of the navigational and blind-bombing radio system upon which the enemy implicitly relied. They had discovered the secrets of Knickebein, but others — like X-Gerät, which already intrigued them — were in the offing. If the British could contrive effective radio countermeasures in time the expected enemy night-bomber offensive, though it might not be defeated, could be seriously frustrated. In order to achieve victory over the enemy night-bombers the British still needed, in the summer of 1940, four types of radar sets, each specifically designed for a particular purpose. These types were: gun-laying (GL) for the anti-aircraft batteries; searchlight control (SLC) for the searchlights; ground-controlled interception (GCI) for overland ground control; and finally Air Interception (AI), airborne radar. Working models of these four kinds of radar were not yet ready, though an airborne radar, AI Mark III, was available, but unreliable.

In the meantime, following on Dr Jones's revelations, it was imperative to organize a means of interfering with Knickebein without a moment's delay. Churchill gave urgent orders to that effect. Counter-measures — jamming stations (and various other devices) — were to have absolute priority. A special unit, No. 80 Wing, was forthwith created, with the task of organizing radio counter-measures. The operation was baptized 'Headache'. It brought a stroke of luck to Wing Commander Edward Addison, who, stuck in an Air Ministry job which he loathed, was now withdrawn from 'Air House' to take command of 80 Wing.

Addison faced an immediate problem. Radio jammers, specifically designed for the job, did not exist. Undeterred, he laid hands on a number of electro-diathermy sets used in hospitals to cauterize wounds. Suitably modified, they could jam the Knickebein wave-band at short range. The diathermy sets were installed in selected police stations. The policeman on duty stood by, and when 80 Wing rang through he switched on. Laughably amateurish as the system was, it was better than nothing.

Addison also commandeered a lot of surplus Lorenz blind-approach transmitters, which he had modified so that they could send out a beam which imitated the dots and dashes and the steady directional note of Knickebein. The phoney British beam would be laid across the Knickebein beam to deceive the enemy bomber and lead it astray. It was a bright idea, but, like the diathermy sets, only worked at short range.

The British wizards were working day and night building a type of scientific radio jammer, cover-named 'Aspirin', and designed to swamp the Knickebein signals. The shortcomings of our night air defences made this job more urgent than any in Britain at the time. It was entrusted to the able hands of Dr

Robert Cockburn at the Telecommunications Research Establishment at Swanage, Dorset. It was to Swanage that my school-mates and I, in the happy days before the war, would sail in the motor-boat *Skylark* from Bournemouth pier. Young as we were, we already believed that England was impregnable, as she had been for nine hundred years against every foe. Now, in 1940, our island stood in imminent danger of invasion.

Cockburn and his team would need some months to turn out 'Aspirin' sets in sufficient numbers. Meanwhile Addison's rudimentary devices would have to do. They were the best that Britain possessed to combat Knickebein bombers.

Addison's 80 Wing was fully engaged on another front of the Wizard War — beacons which like lighthouses sent forth a beam, only an invisible one, to which aircraft could tune in and get a 'fix' of their position. BBC programmes transmitted from stations all over Britain could unwillingly provide the same service; an enemy aircraft had only to tune in to a given programme from a known station and so get a bearing. But the BBC outwitted the enemy by transmitting each programme simultaneously from all its stations. Unable to identify any particular one of them, the Luftwaffe bomber was left, literally, in the dark.

The Luftwaffe could not do without radio beacons; their system of navigation depended on them. They were installed in German-occupied territory from Norway down to western France. They might even be planted by German agents in Britain itself. The British soon found a way of confusing the German beacon network by setting up 'masking beacons' — 'meacons' for short. It was a wicked practical joke; the meacons, scattered judiciously about Britain, picked up the German beacon signals and retransmitted them, thus fooling the German bomber's wireless operator who, unable to distinguish between his own beacon and the meacon, knew not which way to turn.

By 18 August 1940 nine meacon stations were in place. Two days later Addison's strange jumble of electro-diathermy sets and surplus Lorenz transmitters were ready to cope, within their limits, with Knickebein.

7

'WAS NUN?' – 'WHAT NOW?'

It was high time. Two months earlier, on the morrow of France's surrender to the Germans and the flight of General de Gaulle in an RAF transport plane to England, Churchill declared to the world 'Hitler knows that he will have to break us in this island or lose the war.' Heroic, defiant words they were, considering that Britain, the last remaining bastion against Germany's conquering armies and air force, was so poorly armed to withstand the bomber onslaught — the Knockout Blow — not to speak of a possible invasion. Hitler himself was convinced that Germany had already won the war, that Britain would see reason, as he put it, and ask for an armistice.

Indeed, neither Hitler nor his generals had ever seriously thought of a plan to subdue Britain by force. After their crushing victories which ended in France's humiliating defeat in June the army staff asked themselves *'Was nun?'*, what now? Hitler had even ordered the partial demobilization of the Wehrmacht. Churchill's defiance, with the whole of Britain behind him, surely perplexed the Fuehrer, as it did other important people. Pope Pius XII appealed to both sides to make an honourable peace. Charles Lindbergh, the famous American transatlantic pilot, and one of my boyhood heroes, openly declared that Britain was finished; the RAF could not possibly stand up to the Luftwaffe. An attempt at mediation was made by

King Gustav of Sweden, to whom prime minister Churchill replied, insisting that there should be guarantees 'by deeds, not words . . . which would ensure the free and independent life of Czechoslovakia, Poland, Norway, Denmark, Holland, Belgium and above all France.' And that, as far as Churchill was concerned, was that. The question of surrender was never even discussed by him or the cabinet, nor did it occur to the British people.

The frustrated Fuehrer, on the second day of July, had no choice but to decide that an invasion of Britain was 'possible'; 'providing air superiority could be attained'. It would be 'bloody' and 'a horror', he said, but ordered that preparations should begin immediately. The question of air superiority did not particularly bother the Luftwaffe, least of all its blustering commander-in-chief, Hermann Göring. He was boasting that it would take two to four weeks to beat down (*niederschlagen*) the RAF. On 16 July Hitler issued his Directive No. 16: 'Since England in spite of her hopeless military situation shows no signs of coming to an understanding, I have decided to prepare a landing operation and if necessary carry it out . . . .' The aim of the operation, baptized Seelöwe, or 'Sea Lion', was 'to eliminate the English homeland as a base for the prosecution of the war against Germany'.

Three days later, on 19 July, in a speech in the Reichstag Hitler, after directing a string of insults at Churchill, appealed directly to the British people. It was useless to continue the war, he said, and invited the British to be reasonable and give up the struggle. Before the day was out the British people had replied for themselves. The evening newspapers, as well as the BBC, answered with a massive NO. Three days later the foreign secretary, Lord Halifax, officially confirmed that popular response.

By now the Luftwaffe was unleashing its bombers against our coast-bound convoys; mainly in the Channel, but the merchant ships sailing in the North Sea to the Thames estuary and the port of London were not spared. That sector was guarded by a determined band of fighters, among them 85 Squadron. Fierce combats were fought above the sea; the Luftwaffe were heavily punished, but not without casualties on our side. I was one, shot down early one morning into the North Sea and fished out of the water by the good ship *Finisterre*, a trawler out of Hull. I was sodden but unhurt; a change of clothes and a nip of 'oh be joyful' — in the event, rum from the ship's store — was all that was needed to put me back in form for a patrol that evening.

The day battle grew fiercer. The Fuehrer Directive No. 17 of 1 August stated, first, that the Luftwaffe was to overpower the Royal Air Force in the shortest possible time; second, after achieving air superiority, the air war was to be directed against ports and food stores. A sign of things to come; and talking of ports, London was then the biggest in the world.

Göring had set the Grosseinsatz, the main air assault on Britain, for 13 August; the big event had been given in advance the heroic name of Adlertag, Eagle Day. On the eve of Adlertag, the Luftwaffe made a determined attack on certain of the RAF's coastal radar stations, intent on depriving Fighter Command of its early warning system. The vital stations at Poling, Sussex, and Ventnor, Isle of Wight, were put out of action, but the RAF acted astutely, moving into each station a mobile transmitter which deceived the Germans into thinking that the main stations were still working. Three days later Göring told his air commanders that there was no point in continuing the attacks, as the two stations were apparently undamaged. Göring's error, and another he was to make before long, were to lead to the Luftwaffe's undoing.

Eagle Day for the Luftwaffe was something of a flop — order, counter-order, disorder. But it was clear that they were moving inland to attack our airfields. 85 Squadron was now withdrawn from Martlesham on the east coast to Debden, north of London. The 15th and 18th of August were days of furious fighting, with the Luftwaffe losing out heavily. Yet despite their losses the enemy's massed formations kept coming back, ceaselessly pounding the fighter airfields defending our southern ports and farther inland those which stood guard over London itself.

After a fierce but successful fight with a horde of Luftwaffe bombers and fighters on 18 August, 85 squadron was sent forward next day to Croydon, in the Kenley sector covering south London. After a short lull in the fighting, so fierce did the battle then rage that of the score or so of pilots I led to Croydon, fourteen (myself included) were shot down — two of them twice — within the next two weeks. Croydon airfield, already hit three days before our arrival, was soon to be hit again and yet again.

Hitler had reserved to himself personally the order to attack London. Croydon was in the London area, but the daring leader of that first attack, Hauptmann Rubensdorffer, escaped court martial. On the way back he was shot down and he and his gunner killed.

Their massed attacks over for the day, the Luftwaffe sent a small number of their bombers far and wide in the darkness over Britain, bombing scattered targets. Some time before leaving Debden I had been rudely disturbed one night by the rending crash, uncomfortably close, of a 'stick' of bombs. The din was worse than the damage — a few broken windows and one poor rabbit killed by blast. No. 29 Squadron, based at Debden, were doing their best as night-fighters, despite the poor performance of their Blenheim aircraft, with their Mark III AI (radar), and serious problems with the searchlights, who were as ever unable, apparently, to discriminate between our fighters and the enemy. One night a young pilot of 29 Squadron, while stalking an enemy bomber, was caught by the lights. Again and again he called the controller 'Tell them to douse!' but the silvery blue fingers had him in their grasp and would not let go. Struggling to free himself from the blinding flood of light, he lost control of his aircraft. He had left his radio on 'transmit', and his desperate, terrified cries could be heard until the last moment, when his aircraft struck the ground. Another night a Spitfire from a neighbouring squadron, trailing an enemy bomber illuminated by searchlights, unwisely switched on his own headlight and was promptly shot down by the enemy. Much had still to be learned about night-fighting tactics.

In contrast to the Debden raid was the one made by a force of twenty bombers on the Nuffield factory, now tooled up to produce Spitfires, at Castle Bromwich near Birmingham. The bombing was remarkable for its precision, with eleven direct hits.

To oppose the Luftwaffe's night attacks, the RAF's Fighter Command could now put up a small and semi-specialized (it is not possible to say more) night-fighter force. It consisted of six squadrons of Blenheims (29 Squadron included) — converted twin-engined medium bombers fitted with the inefficient Mark III AI radar set and a puny battery of four .303 machine-guns mounted in the nose. In addition to the Blenheims were two squadrons of Defiants — single-engined two-seater fighters with a four-gun (.303) turret in the rear cockpit. Designed originally as day-fighters, Defiants fought valiantly over Dunkirk, and at the outset of the day battle over Britain, but had been decimated. Now they fought at night. Without their own AI radar, the crew, pilot and gunner, had to count on visual sighting. They were called 'cats-eye' night-fighters.

To reinforce this small, determined but ill-equipped night-fighter force the day-fighter squadrons were called upon, if need be, to perform as well as cats-eye fighters. At the close of day, when the enemy cohorts retired and the wearying combats were over, the handful of us who were 'night operational' would stand by for night patrol. 'Goose-neck' flares were laid out to mark the flare-path, but on Croydon's undulating grass patch they provided an uncertain guide, at least for take-off. It was safer to aim just to the right of the red light on the hangar roof. That was the last earthly object you saw as you climbed on up into the darkness. The probing searchlights felt tentatively across the sky for the enemy, but rarely succeeded in illuminating him for the benefit of the searching fighters.

Very seldom indeed were the enemy raiders intercepted by our night-fighters. A Heinkel, however, did manage to get itself shot down at the end of July, near Newbury — and all credit to the fighter. Their unfortunate adventure led one of the crew, the *beobachter* (observer) into an even more extraordinary one. A man of considerable resource, he remained at large for nine days, nibbling a chocolate bar and gnawing roots pulled up from the fields at night. By day he hid in the woods among bracken and scrub. While he was dozing beneath a tree, a red handkerchief over his face, two men passed within thirty yards of him, but did not see him. When another Englishman (out pigeon-shooting) approached, the German shinned up the nearest tree, holding his breath as the man and his dog walked by below.

When Sunday came the *beobachter*, perched high in his tree, observed many a young couple strolling in the wood. He envied them, for his own young wife was expecting a baby. Another night in the wood, and he was by then so weak from hunger that he decided to give himself up. He walked to the nearest road. A young couple came bicycling by, but the moment they saw him they pedalled on furiously. Then came a car, luxurious and shining. It slowed down, passed him, then backed. The rear door opened and the distinguished-looking lady inside opened the rear door and beckoned to him to enter: 'Get in, my good man, and sit down,' said Lady Buckland, tapping with her hand the plush seat beside her. Astonished by her gentleness and courtesy, the German airman obeyed, muttering half-ashamed *'Polizei, bitte.'* 'To the police station!' her ladyship ordered her chauffeur, and there this unlikely couple took leave of each other.

Between us, the radar fighters seeing but dimly in the dark with their short-sighted and unreliable Mark III AI and we, the cats-eye fighters, straining our eyes into the night (helped or more often hindered by the searchlights) were in no such state to fight the Luftwaffe's night bombers as we were to tackle their day bombers. Happily, Headache and the meacons were ready, and Aspirin was on the way. Happily, too, the people of London and Britain's provincial cities were braced for the onslaught.

CASUALTY

In the early hours of 24 August the whistle and crash of falling bombs rent the darkness of Croydon. They narrowly missed the pilots' quarters, where I was fitfully dozing, and set ablaze two of our Hurricanes. One had just been delivered, sparkling new, with all the latest fittings; we were well rid of the other, known in the vernacular as a 'clapped-out old shag-bag'. The Croydon raid was yet another infringement of the Fuehrer's personal orders, but not nearly so flagrant as the attack which that same night blasted the very heart of the City of London. The raid on London was unintentional: the Luftwaffe crews involved, ordered to bomb oil tanks at Rochester and Thameshaven, downstream from the City, had overshot their target; they were severely disciplined on their return. Hitler, still believing that the British would be 'reasonable' and surrender, did not wish to provoke them. But the Fuehrer's go-softly attitude towards Britain was wrecked by those bombs on the City of London. The following night, on Churchill's order, the RAF retaliated with bombs on Berlin. They dropped leaflets too, saying 'the war which Hitler started will go on . . . as long as Hitler does.' But it was the bombs which had the most stunning effect on Berliners. Remembering Göring's crack 'If ever a bomb drops on Germany, you can call me Meier', that is what Berliners were now doing.

'Hammer at the enemy day and night to break his nerve', Göring ordered his Luftwaffe. By day the RAF's fighter bases around London were being so battered that, with buildings shattered and telephone wires cut, they had to move out to emergency operations rooms, away from the base. The Kenley ops. room was set up anew in a local butcher's shop.

The Luftwaffe's night offensive was mounting too. On the night of 28 August came their first mass night-attack. They chose the great docks at Liverpool and Birkenhead as their target. For three nights they returned to attack the docks; Blenheim night-fighters and cats-eye fighters were dispatched to intercept, but the bombers got through unscathed. Most bomber crews on their return reported hits on the target. But German air reconnaissance photos did not confirm all their claims; a mass of bombs had fallen wide of the docks. Was the RAF, the German crews wondered, interfering somehow with their aim?

The answer, which was soon to become abundantly clear, was yes. 80 Wing, with its Headache, Aspirin and Meacons, was sowing confusion among the Luftwaffe's bombers where guns and fighters had failed. Many hits, the German air photos showed, fell on what was obviously a decoy fire well south of the docks. The British called them 'Starfish' sites. The ruse had been employed by the Germans themselves; now their own aircrews were being deceived in the same way.

While the Luftwaffe were showering bombs on Liverpool and its environs, RAF Bomber Command were again over Berlin. Ten people were killed, and a cry went up from the German press against the brutality of the British in killing women and children. 'Cowardly British Attack!' 'British air pirates over Berlin!'

The outrage of the Nazi chiefs was only exceeded by their hypocrisy. It was the German Air Force which had first bombed London in 1915, proving that civilian non-combatants were henceforth in the front line, potential if not legitimate victims of what Churchill called 'this cursed, hellish invention and development of air power'. The Luftwaffe had massacred civilians at Guernica, Warsaw and Rotterdam. Now the Germans were getting a small taste of their own medicine, but before terrible retribution was to overtake them British cities and above all London had first to submit to the hellfire of Luftwaffe air-raids. Already during August they had killed over a thousand civilians, nearly half of them women and children.

While the Luftwaffe were attacking more and more strategic targets under cover of darkness, during the daytime it was throwing everything it could into an all-out effort to destroy the RAF day-fighter bases defending London. On 30 and 31 August the day battle reached an unprecedented ferocity. The 31st was our blackest day, when 39 pilots were killed and many more shot down and wounded. Such losses may sound trifling, but there were not all that many of us, and our ranks, particularly among the leaders, were seriously breached.

I was one of the casualties on the 31st. As Dornier bombers swept over Croydon, demolishing hangars and technical buildings, I led my squadron off through the smoke and dust against the attackers. Twenty minutes later, after a sharp cut-and-thrust combat with a swarm of escorting Messerschmitts, my Hurricane was hit. So was I. Once again my parachute saved me. That night in Croydon General Hospital the surgeon took a 20mm cannon-shell out of my foot. As I passed out under the anaesthetic I could faintly hear the sirens wailing. The Luftwaffe were closing in on London.

9

ZIELWECHSEL – TARGET CHANGE

Both Fighter Command and the Luftwaffe were being stretched to the limit of endurance, in men and in machines. Never before (or since) did Fighter Command hurl against the enemy, time and time again, so many of its fighters as during those two white-hot days of fighting — and never at greater cost. Pilot casualties on our side were now catastrophic, far exceeding the output from the training schools. Worse, as experienced pilots were numerous among the dead and wounded, the gaps they left had to be filled by raw lads with no battle experience.

1 September was a bad day for Fighter Command, a disastrous one for 85 Squadron. Led by its one remaining flight commander, Patrick Woods-Scawen, it lost four pilots including Patrick. On 3 September the squadron was withdrawn from the front line and sent to Church Fenton in Yorkshire, led this time by Sammy Allard, who (still a non-commissioned officer) was the Squadron's best pilot. All this time I lay helpless in my hospital bed; Tim Moloney, our faithful adjutant, came in every day to tell me the news.

The Luftwaffe's assaults on fighter airfields continued unabated, until on 3 September — apart from the rubble and ruin on the ground — we had daily losses in the air (which hitherto had not exceeded the Luftwaffe's) equal, with sixteen down on each side. It looked to Field Marshal 'Smiling Albert' Kesselring, commanding Luftflotte 2, as if the British fighter force was *kaput*. Moreover, that same day RAF reconnaissance planes photographed over 4000 invasion craft assembled in French ports. Yet to Hermann Göring, whom Hitler had ordered to crush the RAF, it was evident that the RAF was so far uncrushable. Fighter Command, though badly diminished, was still fighting back. Bomber Command were attacking Berlin and lashing out nightly against the German invasion fleet − to the discomfort of the Kriegsmarine upon whom Hitler was counting to transport his invasion troops to England's shores.

With a decisive victory over the RAF's fighters still eluding him, Göring believed that his last hope was to launch a mass assault on London, the world's biggest and most prestigious target. In defence of the capital, the Reichsmarschall figured, every available British fighter would be forced into the air where the German *Jäger* would round them up and destroy them. Such a world-shattering success, Göring comforted himself, would incidentally give a badly needed lift to his ego, subdued these recent weeks by the failure of his Luftwaffe.

Kesselring gave his enthusiastic support to Göring's plan; he had been pressing for some time for an all-out attack on London. But General Sperrle, commanding Luftflotte 3, disagreed as usual with Kesselring. 'Continue to attack their fighter bases by day', he argued, 'and by night, the London docks'. His strategy, had it been followed, might well have given the Luftwaffe victory over the RAF fighters. But Göring, who had already made one fatal error in sparing the RAF's radar stations, and Kesselring, an ex-soldier ill versed in air strategy, prevailed. London was to be the Luftwaffe's new target; plans for the *Zielwechsel* (target change) now went urgently ahead. The attack on London was code-named Loge, after the god who forged Siegfried's sword. It only remained for the Fuehrer to put the new offensive across to the German public.

This he did on 4 September, at the opening of the *Winterhilfe* (winter help) campaign, before an audience of women, in the Sportpalast in Berlin. With heavy sarcasm, he turned to the question that everyone was asking: when will England be invaded? 'England will collapse', he told the excited ladies, 'and if people in England are asking "Why doesn't he come?" I reply "Don't worry, he is coming."'

On that vexatious problem of the RAF's night attacks on the capital, the Fuehrer reassured his audience: 'We are now answering, night for night . . . we will raze their cities to the ground.' He ended with a repetition of his old theme: 'The hour will come when one of us will go under, and it will not be National Socialist Germany.' 'Never, never!' came the frenzied response. Next day Hitler confirmed the order for 'attacks on the inhabitants and air defences of British cities, including London'.

Though Fighter Command's chief, Air Chief Marshal Dowding, was of course ignorant of the Fuehrer's order, it was to prove the answer to his prayer. On 6 September the plight of his fighter force was desperate. Six out of the seven sector airfields and five advanced landing grounds in 11 Group, which stood guard between London and the Luftwaffe bases across the Channel, were badly damaged. Losses of fighter aircraft largely exceeded production, and reserves were running low. The output of new pilots could not keep pace with battle losses; the little company of fighter pilots, originally about a thousand, had dwindled to about seven hundred. Victory was in the Luftwaffe's grasp, but a miracle was about to happen. The morrow would tell.

The morning and afternoon of 7 September were quiet. Then towards 5.30 p.m. massed bomber formations, heavily escorted by fighters advanced not as expected on the fighter airfields, but direct on London.

At No. 1 Helen Street, Woolwich, thirteen-year-old Ray Callow was with his six-year-old nephew Evan, a pink-faced, fair-haired boy, the son of Ray's sister Rose, who was at work in the Arsenal. Mrs Callow had gone shopping — she always left it till the evening, when prices were cheaper. The two boys were alone, busy putting a model aeroplane together — Ray, the expert, was happy that Evan was already becoming an enthusiast.

As they worked with glue and balsa wood, Ray became aware

of a murmur of voices coming from the street, and through the window saw crowds gathered outside looking eastward up into the sky. Almost immediately, from the direction of Woolwich Common, came the *whoomf, whoomf* of anti-aircraft fire — it frightened Ray at first, for he had never heard the guns so close. All the same, he took little Evan by the hand, and with no thought for the danger of falling shell-splinters the two young model-aircraft enthusiasts walked outside to join the crowd. Like everyone else, Ray looked eastward downstream towards the estuary. Never had he seen such a terrifying sight; the sky was dotted with a mass of specks which seemed to be quite motionless. Then as he realized they were approaching, he recognized them as Heinkels and Dorniers, flanked by escorts of Messerschmitt 109s and 110s. The boys could not imagine there could be so many at once. In fact the Luftwaffe had amassed nearly four hundred bombers and more than six hundred fighters — over a thousand aircraft — for this all-out attack. After crossing the English coast they had borne down straight on London. This was the curtain-raiser of Loge, the knock-out blow on the capital. A year had passed since we had waited for it, basking in the sun beside our machines at Tangmere.

Ray stood mesmerized by the sight of this vast phalanx of aircraft, formation after formation, stepped up one behind the other like a giant staircase mounting in the sky from 16,000 to 30,000 feet. Now they were moving visibly closer to London — and him. But still he stood rooted there, holding Evan's hand, his eyes fixed on the awe-inspiring horde. British fighters were swooping on the bombers, scything through them and jousting with the enemy fighters. Vapour trails were tracing white circles and criss-crossing against the blue background of the sky, smeared here and there by black smoke from smitten aircraft, German and British. Ray watched horrified as a Messerschmitt 109, one wing shorn off, fell twisting crazily to earth. After it came a Spitfire, its pilot apparently aiming to crash-land on Woolwich Common. The Spit did not make it. It hit the road somewhere in front of the long façade of the Gunners' Mess with a huge explosion which sent the pilot's body hurtling through a fence of corrugated iron. (The fence was patched up with a new sheet of iron which for years remained as a local landmark.)

Watching from outside her denture workshop in Woolwich, Ray's sister Melve (an adventurous spirit like him) had seen the wingless Me109 crash and ran off, glad to put some distance between herself and the bombing. She found the wreckage of the German fighter lying in the back garden of a terraced house through which the curious had first to pass. She threw the few pennies she had on her into a bucket outside the front door marked 'For the Spitfire Fund'. She came to the back garden and the wreckage of the Messerschmitt. In its cockpit there lolled the dead body of the pilot, one of his arms hanging limply outside. Melve was immediately struck by the slender fingers, the manicured nails. Round his neck was wrapped a bright silk scarf, and looking at his young face Melve could not believe that a dead man could look so handsome. 'He must be from the wealthy class', she thought, this girl from the poorer class, now caught up in 'total war', a wholesale slaughter which showed no respect for 'class' or non-combatants.

The massed bombers were now nearly above where Ray was watching, and the air reverberated with the steady throb of their engines. Then suddenly above the thunder there came the whining crescendo of falling bombs, crashing down into the heart of London's dockland. Ray, gripping Evan's hand, said 'It's time we went inside.' Closing the door of No. 1 behind them, the two boys crawled under the dining-room table, as they had always been told to do.

The Dornier 17 *Gustav Marie* of KG2 was flying in the serried formations of that aerial armada. Its wireless operator, Unteroffizier Werner Borner, looked down through the billowing columns of smoke at the chaos of fire and explosions below. As British fighters cut their way through the escorting Messerschmitts to attack the bombers, it was impossible, said Borner, to tell friend from foe. The Dornier released its bombs, and Borner saw them go down 'on the exact spot' — the Royal Victoria and the Royal Albert docks on the north bank of the Thames.

Just opposite, on the south bank, smoke belched from the

German-owned Siemens cable works – ironic, for the RAF had hit their factory in Berlin. Further downstream, in the streets of Woolwich, the cry went up 'The Arsenal's been hit!' A conflagration was raging within the confines of its 120-acre site; bombs had blasted and set fire to workshops and stacks of containers full of nitro-glycerine, dumps of small-arms ammunition and heavy shells which were exploding and careering wildly into the air. Clanging fire bells, ack-ack guns, bursting bombs, the diving and zooming and the steady thunder of aircraft overhead increased the shindy to an unimaginable pitch. Yet apparently the Arsenal's Danger Buildings, where Johnny's wife Kathleen worked, had survived, for it was common opinion that if the Danger Buildings went up half of London would go up too.

As Ray watched the leaping flames and writhing columns of grey-black smoke mounting skyward he could not believe that somewhere in the midst of that holocaust were his sisters Amy and Rose; and Kathleen, Johnny's wife, and Alf his brother. His mind went blank at the thought, and he could only pray that they had taken to the shelters or the open ground. He thought of his brother Bert, manning his balloon site up on Woolwich Common; he should be all right. But his father? That morning Ray had as usual brought him a lunch packet of steak and kidney pudding and dumplings. In the heavy-gun shop where Mr Callow worked the heat was so intense that the men could not simply run out straight into the open air. They had to cool off gradually. For them no escape to the shelters; they had to stay put while the bombs rained down. Ray refused to think that any harm might have befallen his father. He had always believed him to be indestructible, and still did.

The boy's thoughts turned to his oldest brother, Johnny – the ballroom dancer turned fireman. No doubt he was somewhere in the thick of the fire-fighting. Johnny, like most of the volunteers in the Auxiliary Fire Service, had so far not seen a big fire. The regulars of the London Fire Brigade would always go in first, and the AFS would merely follow to clean up the mess. But neither had the regulars even seen fires such as those that raged that day in east London.

10

LONDON ON FIRE

During the morning Johnny had been sitting around reading and chatting with his comrades in the common room at the sub-station at Earldom Square, Eltham. Their station was once a school which had been evacuated. The assembly hall served as a common-room for the firemen; the classrooms had been converted into dormitories. Outside waited their ten pumps mounted on two wheels and painted grey. Their fire-fighting apparatus bore no resemblance to the familiar red fire-engine with its extensible ladder. The ten pumps of the Earldom sub-station were each towed by a London taxi. Occasionally private cars, even big, luxurious Buicks and Chryslers (though these were less manœuvrable) would be used as towing vehicles.

The taxi carried a team of four men: No. 1 — the leading fireman — that was Johnny's role. He sat up front next to No. 2, the driver. Nos. 3 and 4 sat on the back seat.

Around 4 p.m. a Yellow warning had come through from Fire Headquarters at Lambeth, via 37 area HQ at New Cross and the main station at Avery Hill (another requisitioned school) down to the Earldom Square sub-station. The Yellow was soon followed by a Red, which signalled that the raid had crossed the coast. Outside in the streets, air-raid wardens were warning people to go to their Anderson shelters in the garden or to public shelters. Those who could not make it were shepherded into the warden's post, solidly protected by sandbags. By now the atmosphere was tense — everybody was waiting for the bombs to fall.

Tons of them had already gone down into the docks north and south of the river, and a heavy pall of smoke was spreading towards Woolwich. Suddenly the girl on the switchboard at Earldom Square received the order: Eight pumps to the Arsenal! She pressed down eight of the ten buttons (one for each pump), and threw a switch which set the alarm bell pealing. Leading Fireman Johnny Callow with the seven other No. 1s rushed to the control room to get final details, while the remaining members of each team made for their 'pump' (the expression included the towing taxi) in which all their equipment was already stowed — long rubber boots, axes, helmets, gas-masks and blue tunics with silvery buttons. Like the others, Johnny's pump was already moving off when he came dashing from the control-room, jumped aboard and took his place next to the driver. Then they were tearing through the streets and as they went, pulling on their long boots and uniform coat, adjusting their tin hat — all except No. 2, the driver. He would have to wait till they arrived at the fire.

On the way there the men were silent. Johnny felt his tummy turning, and he knew the others felt the same. Then he spoke: 'Well, mates, we've all got the wind up properly, haven't we? So grit your teeth — this is the job we're paid for, even if it's only three quid a week.'

Johnny's pump reached Beresford Square, next to the Arsenal main gates, just as the first bombs were falling. Pumps from other stations were queuing to get in and when Johnny's pump entered, the place was a tempest of fire, shooting sparks and exploding bombs. In the suffocating smoke they could hardly breathe, let alone see.

This time it was the real thing, the test of all their months of training. Each man knew exactly what to do. The taxi came to a halt near a hydrant and the four men jumped out. Johnny, No. 1, strode forward towards the fire to get orders from the control officer; he moved with the ballroom dancer's step, heel and toe. It was second nature to him, and all his comrades' teasing would never change it. Back he strode to his pump, where No. 2 had already started up the motor; Nos. 3 and 4 had run out the connecting hose and stand-pipe and joined them up to the hydrant. They were back at the pump, unloading the eight reels of hose and connecting them together. Johnny directing, the two men ran the hose out towards a blazing stack of nitro-glycerine containers; they advanced, both of them holding the 'branch', the brass nozzle which was adjusted to throw a fan jet to protect them as they closed in. Then Johnny gave the order 'Let 'er go!' and the men, taking a firmer grip of the branch, adjusted it to give a power jet. They felt as if they were fighting with a rearing horse. Holding down the branch with all their strength, they aimed the jet so that its deluge of water fell full upon the flames, damping them down into clouds of steam and acrid smoke.

Johnny and his No. 2 took five minutes off for a cup of tea and a sandwich. They had not far to go; the Salvation Army's mobile canteens were on the spot, and young men and women in their blue uniform and tin hats were handing out refreshments: ''Ere, guv'nor, a cupper and a sandwich . . .' Johnny admired them; they had ventured as close as they dared to the fire, and were indefatigable as they served the fire-fighters. He and his mate swallowed down their tea and sandwich, then went to take over from the men on the branch; it was now their turn for a break.

The fading daylight brought no reprieve to the firemen. Night bombers were streaming up the estuary towards London. Hauptmann Hajo Hermann, piloting a Junkers 88 bomber, remarked: 'A very clear night. Everything was lit up by fires, like a huge torch in the night.' Until that night Luftwaffe aircrews had obeyed strict orders against indiscriminate bombing. Now they simply tipped their bombs into the sea of flame and smoke below.

Since the beginning of the attack at 5.30 that evening more than fifty pumps had come to the Arsenal's rescue. They had been fighting, regardless of the ceaseless bombardment, for four hours. Now it was getting on for 10 p.m. and more pumps came in to relieve them. Johnny's team was ordered to knock off, 'make up' and return to the sub-station.

The Callow family, most of them shaken, but all unhurt, had gathered at No. 1 Helen Street that evening. The old man was still missing and Renée, the youngest daughter, was on duty as usherette at the Granada cinema. In the middle of the evening performance a near miss blasted open the Granada's doors. People started to hurry out into the street, only to find it blocked by broken glass and rubble. Back they trooped inside shepherded by the manager and usherettes, who soon had them going in a rollicking sing-song.

At that moment Renée's sister Melve, escorted by her brother Alf, was approaching the Granada. Alf, not yet seventeen, had nevertheless wangled his way into the Home Guard, and proudly wore the khaki uniform and forage cap. He had insisted on accompanying Melve on her risky errand. When the bombs struck the two were knocked flat and covered with dust. Alf, the gallant but untried soldier, passed clean out under the shock, and rescue men searching for the dead and wounded loaded his recumbent body into an ambulance. Melve, now on her feet again and brushing the dust from her hair and clothes, suddenly noticed what was going on. 'Hey!' she shouted, 'that bloke's me bloomin' brother. There's nothing wrong with him!' Alf was pulled unceremoniously out of the ambulance and dumped on the ground. A minute later he and Melve were threading their way through the debris to deliver Renée's supper.

It was around 8 p.m. that a tall, heavily built man presented himself at the door of the Callows' home. Ray opened the door. Before him stood an apparition, the hair singed off its head; its body — half-naked in the tattered remains of a boiler suit — was black from head to foot. 'It's Dad,' said Mr Callow. 'Not many of us got out alive when the big-gun shop was hit. I've walked back, but I feel a bit groggy.'

Mr Callow was badly shell-shocked. Ray helped him upstairs to the bath-tub. 'You can leave me, mate', Mr Callow told his son, then turned on the cold tap — there was no hot water. Within half an hour he had washed himself down and changed into clean clothes. He told Ray, 'Now I'm slipping down to the Bull for one or two.'

By the time he was back Ray had left for the Town Hall to report for duty. Clad in Scout's uniform, pepper-coloured plimsolls and tin hat with initials ARP on it, he felt very proud of being able to help in the defence of his country. The waxing moon had risen, its feeble light only occasionally visible through the pall of smoke that hung over Woolwich. In one hand Ray held a dimmed-out pocket torch, though he rarely used it, knowing the streets as he did like the back of his hand. There was a sharp nip in the air, and he walked on briskly, noticing that although the terraced houses were apparently not hit, the windows of all of them, like those of his own home, had been blown in. The occupants of those houses would be shivering that night.

It was getting on for 9 o'clock when Ray reached Beresford Square, still choked with fire-pumps and ambulances, the former pressing forward towards the fires, the latter going in and coming away with the injured. Yet despite the confusion and the ceaseless rain of bombs, the food stalls of the 'Squareheads' were still open, with customers queuing to make their last purchases and reasoning that as long as the costermongers stood their ground they had better do so too, or lose their place in the queue. 'Business as usual' was the watchword of these extraordinary, resistant people. Ray threaded his way among them amazed, not least at himself. They had all known for months that they were going to get it in the neck sooner or later. Yet now, though slightly dazed by the weight and horror of the bombardment, they still did not seem to realize fully the disaster that had befallen them.

Ray was unperturbed by the drone of bombers overhead and the din of bombs below. He walked on, and came to the Town Hall where he reported for duty at the ARP Headquarters in the basement below. For the next three hours he dashed here and there carrying tea and sandwiches, and the occasional message, to the men and women of the civil defence and the heavy-rescue squads as they hacked and picked and shovelled away in the debris, searching for survivors. Ray felt there was nothing more worthwhile, and exciting too, than to be able to help these brave men. Their faces and arms were covered with dust and sweat (and sometimes blood) as they toiled away in their filthy blue overalls, hailing each other as 'mate' and 'guv'nor' and despite the macabre scene cracking an occasional joke. Though relieved by a new shift in the early hours of the 8th, they refused to leave, so the work went ahead at double the pace.

It was not until well after midnight that young Ray reported back to HQ at the Town Hall. The duty warden thanked him with 'Off you go, mate, and get some sleep.' Half an hour later the boy flopped onto his bed in No. 1 Helen Street. The Callow family had had a basketful that day — and Johnny was still fighting the fires.

After receiving the order to knock-off from their four-hour battle with the fires at the Arsenal, Johnny and his team got back to the substation, their clothes soaked through, their faces and hands begrimed. They straightway washed down and changed into dry clothing. Before they had time for a cup of tea and a sandwich, the alarm bell pealed again. 'All pumps to the Surrey Commercial Docks!'

As they raced through the streets — lit up here and there by a burning house — they were tempted to stop and extinguish the fire. But the orders were 'Surrey Commercial Docks', where at the Canadian Dock a conflagration was devouring some million tons of pinewood, sending flames and sparks flying hundreds of feet into the sky. When a wooden partition stood in the firemen's way a burly Canadian lumberjack appeared from nowhere and with his long axe laid on furiously at the obstacle and hacked it down. The firemen advanced some way under the protection of their 'fan-jet'. Then they readjusted the branch, and the power-jet, under hundreds of pounds to the square inch of pressure, tore into the flames. This was going to be a long and exhausting fight.

But the Salvation Army and other volunteers like the

Women's Volunteer Service (WVS) were as usual at the rendezvous. Johnny swore that without their aid the firemen could never have held on as they did, with an occasional cup of tea and a sandwich, until six o'clock next morning.

It was only then that the last of the Luftwaffe night-bombers was on its way back to base. London had endured a ceaseless bombardment lasting twelve hours, the like of which no other city on earth had yet suffered — not Guernica, nor Warsaw or Rotterdam. The day battle was not yet over, but the night battle had begun. Among the smoke and ruins of London that morning of Sunday the 8th, 430 Londoners lay dead — nearly as many as the fighter pilots killed during all the four months of the day battle, the 'Battle of Britain'. This was only the first night of London's agony; the capital was yet to endure, night after night and without respite, another two months of mass attacks.

11
INVASION POSTPONED

That Sunday morning, although the flames had been subdued, clouds of smoke still drifted over Woolwich. Mr Callow was still feeling far from himself, yet he was up betimes as usual, making tea for the family. He brought Ray a cup. 'Listen, me lad,' he told his son, 'I'll not be around for a week. Doctor's orders.' Ray smiled but said nothing. He had never admired his father more. He would miss him, but it would not be long before he was back.

Young Ray had made daring plans for that day. He swallowed down his tea, dressed and left the house, making for the Woolwich free ferry; its skipper, Captain Hudson, had been plying back and forth across the Thames during the previous night, steering between flaming barges, bringing refugees, clinging to their belongings — which included cats, dogs, white mice and parrots — from Canning Town and Silvertown on the north bank. Rumour had it that those two places had been burnt to the ground, and Ray (as if he had not already seen enough at Woolwich) was curious to find out how things looked on the other side of the river.

He stepped off the ferry at North Woolwich on the opposite bank and made his way through the smoking ruins of Silvertown, past the royal group of docks — Victoria, Albert, where Borner's bombs had struck, and the George V docks. When he came to Canning Town fires were still burning. In the shambles of burnt and shattered masonry he suddenly came upon scores of one-pound notes scattered in the street. Ray stopped dead. He had but one thought: don't touch! Run for it. He ran all the way back to the ferry, crossed to the south bank and kept running until he reached home. Breathlessly he told his mother about the pound notes. 'You didn't touch anything, did you?' 'No, Mum, honest I didn't,' answered Ray. She believed him; he was a good boy, better than others she had heard of who would have made off with such easy loot.

Following its gigantic effort, the Luftwaffe laid off during the day. Göring, in his special train *Asia*, with its cooks and servants and its stocks of wine and food, was now in personal command, as the German radio solemnly announced. Pleased with the destruction wrought by his Luftwaffe, he warmed to his task of destroying London. He was convinced that sustained attacks would lead to a crack in the morale of Londoners. Hitler, fed by Göring's rosy reports, thought the same; he had been obsessed by the British refusal to surrender. But now he had lifted his ban on attacking London — 'a stroke at the enemy's heart'. He was sure, he informed his generals, that this would create mass hysteria and revolution with the people pleading for an armistice. He was only as wrong as the Luftwaffe's chief.

Göring that day divided London into two zones: A, East London and B, West London. The 'West-End' with its railway termini and power-stations was to be as fair game as the 'East-End' and its docks and warehouses. With a laughably naïve act of generalship, he ordered that the main effort that night was to be concentrated on Kensington, Buckingham Palace and West Ham. London again suffered cruelly; 412 civilians died, half of them women and children. Next morning's *Völkischer Beobachter* reported, with cynical falsehood, 'attacks against military and economic targets by strong forces and the heaviest bombs.' The heaviest of them all was the 'Satan', whose blast was effective 500 yards away.

When in the late afternoon of the 9th the Luftwaffe returned to the assault on London they were in for a surprise. London's brave action in drawing the enemy's fire from the fighter airfields had enabled the RAF to make a remarkable recovery. The German fighter leader, Hauptmann Hannes Trautloft, at the head of Jagdgeschwader 54, reported: 'The sky was full of roundels; for the first time we had the feeling we were outnumbered.' The raiders were repulsed, the German High Command nonplussed by the unflagging resistance of the British fighters.

But after nightfall the bombers were back in force. There were 370 Londoners slain, 1400 badly injured. The *Völkischer Beobachter* rejoiced next day: 'London witnesses a morning of terror after 9½ hours of air raid.' Valiant London. During the daytime the British fighters still fought to protect her. But by night the capital lay wide open to attack. The night-fighters, with unreliable radar, or none at all, searched vainly in the dark for the assailants. Nor were the Ack-Ack guns and searchlights (themselves without radar) able to stem the incoming tide of bombers.

The day did not go so well on the 11th for the RAF's day-fighters, who had to fight through the enemy's screen of escorting Messerschmitts before closing with the bombers. One of these, a Heinkel of KG26, provided some comic relief to the murderous combats. Hit by Spitfires, it dropped out of formation. The pilot shouted orders to the crew to bale out, and dived out himself through the front hatch. The other three of the crew were made of sterner stuff; they stuck to their ship. The observer, grabbing the abandoned controls, yelled 'Jettison everything!' Some minutes later watchers in the Tunbridge Wells area were intrigued to see an unusual object descending towards them. It fell at their feet — a full-dress Luftwaffe uniform, complete with Iron Cross, ceremonial dagger and in one pocket shaving tackle and toilet requisites, which had floated down on a coat-hanger from the heavens. The owner, Unteroffizier Schilling, wireless operator, with his two companions, managed to limp back to base in their badly damaged Heinkel.

After the day's fighting hopes rose again in Berlin. To the German High Command it looked as if the British fighters were at last on the verge of defeat. This brought little joy to the Kriegsmarine; that night, after attacks by Royal Navy light craft and RAF bombers, the invasion ports of Ostend, Dunkirk, Calais and Boulogne were declared 'completely unsafe'.

The same could be said of certain districts in London, once again the target that night of a mass attack. Luftwaffe bombers, mingling with the stream of returning RAF bombers, greatly confused the British coastal radar. Not that it made any difference to our night-fighters or ack-ack guns, who, with or without coastal radar, and without any of their own, were helpless to protect the capital.

To Londoners the guns did, however, sound more aggressive than usual. Indeed, their meagre numbers had been doubled by reinforcements from the provincial cities. The ceaseless din of gunfire gave the people heart. 'Now we're giving it back to them!' they thought, and felt all the better. Young Ray imagined that in that appalling shindy enemy bombers were plunging earthward, victims of both guns and night-fighters. But that night the 13,500 shells fired by the guns did nothing, any more than did the night-fighters, to cause the imagined slaughter among the enemy, who admired the fireworks from a safe height. And not everyone in London appreciated this increased tumult of noise. It terrified children and their mothers and, more than the bombs, disturbed the sleep of those innocents.

Grey nimbus clouds and blessed rain during the day of 12 September brought relief to London. Among those who welcomed the lull was Unteroffizier Karl Missy, whose Heinkel I had shot down near Whitby seven months ago. He had been transferred to the Royal Albert Hospital at Woolwich, reserved for wounded German airmen. Poor Karl — for him and his comrades it was out of the frying-pan into the fire. In his hospital bed he lay, a helpless target for the bombs of his *liebe kamaraden*. When the sirens started wailing three cigarettes were handed to each prisoner. But now they were wailing so often that cigarettes were in short supply.

More and more Luftwaffe prisoners kept arriving at the hospital. Invasion, they told their comrades, would be any day now. Hitler would soon be in London. Encouraging news for Karl, lying in bed with the risk of being killed by German bombs!

When the air-raid warning sounded soldiers would enter the ward and stand guard, one at the end of each bed. As the bombs came crashing closer the guards would dive under the bed, whose occupant would lean over and inquire, 'How are you, there below?', only to be answered by a string of oaths. The nurses alone remained faithful to their duty.

It was the same with the nurses at Croydon General Hospital, twelve miles away from Karl Missy, where I myself was confined to bed, unable to walk. There the bombardment was not so fierce, but we had our share, with splinters shattering the windows and strewing the floor of the ward. Serene and smiling, the nurses would come and hold our hands, telling us, the supposed heroes of the battle, not to be afraid.

The lull on the 12th was short-lived. During the hours of darkness, while single enemy bombers ranged as far as Merseyside, a large force again concentrated on London.

All day long on the 13 September German radio stations kept blaring bellicose tunes like *Wir fliegen gegen England* and *Bomben auf Eng-el-and*, working the public up into a fever of expectancy. The Wehrmacht and the Kriegsmarine were ready to sail. Göring had fixed a date for victory day. Yet Hitler was in a quandary: to invade or not to invade? That was the question tormenting him. But Göring was reassuring: leave everything to me and my Luftwaffe; the attacks on London had produced a terrific effect. Even Buckingham Palace had been hit; though Göring did not know it, the King and Queen escaped death by a few yards. Queen Elizabeth was now able to say, 'We feel we can look the East End of London straight in the face.' These were hard days — and nights — for Londoners of all sorts and conditions.

Göring felt confident. 'British nerves', he told his Fuehrer, 'are at cracking point. The RAF has only fifty Spitfires left' (he made no mention of Hurricanes, which had done even greater execution). Hitler cheered up. The air battle, according to Göring, was going so well that there was now no need for invasion. That night he sent another mass raid to London — one more red-hot nail, he imagined, in the British coffin.

On the 14th Admiral Raeder, chief of the Kriegsmarine, submitted his own views, far more objective than Göring's, to the Fuehrer. 'The present air situation does not allow the undertaking of Sea Lion' (the cover name for invasion). Hitler, not altogether freed from Göring's spell, reacted: 'Four or five more days of fine weather and we have a good chance of forcing England to her knees.' Yet there still remained one snag which exasperated the Fuehrer. 'The enemy keeps on coming back,' he observed. But still, even if it would need as many as ten or twelve days to liquidate the British fighters, the chances were, he predicted, that the British public might meanwhile succumb to mass hysteria.

Thus the German Fuehrer. The British Prime Minister saw things otherwise. 'The attacks on London were for us a breathing space of which we had the utmost need.'

However, Fighter Command's defence had been scrappy that day: fourteen aircraft down on each side. In Berlin, hopes of eliminating the RAF fighters were still high. 'Four or five more days . . .' The Fuehrer agreed that preparations for Sea Lion should continue. 'A new order will follow on the 17th,' he promised. Meanwhile the Luftwaffe were all set for a supreme effort on the morrow. It was to deliver the coup de grâce to Fighter Command.

Not long after sunset the night bombers were back as usual, with impunity, to give London another pounding. Just before it started the Callows received an unexpected visitor, an official of the Home Office, formally clad in black jacket, striped trousers and bowler hat. After a day spent with the Woolwich civil authorities it was now too late for him to get back to London. The Town Hall had sent him to the Callows, who received him hospitably and showed him up to a spare room on the third floor. Before the night was far gone the Callows and their guest were to have a narrow escape which, at least for that incorrigible London family, ended in a good laugh.

Despite the bombs and the admonitions of the ARP wardens,

the Callows, like thousands of others, never went to the shelters at night. They preferred to sleep at home in their own beds, come what may. And so it was that Melve was awakened in the night by a weird flapping noise. It sounded as if scores of wet sheets were being shaken out. The noise came closer, then ended abruptly with a vague bump and a clatter, maybe of tiles. Melve turned over and dropped off to sleep again.

Early next morning she left the house to fetch the Sunday paper. She did notice that the roof of the tall house (once notorious as a gambling den) on the other side of the narrow street looked a bit odd, but thought no more of it. On her way back, dawdling as she read the headlines, she looked up again at the house opposite. Only then did she realize that there was a big hole in the roof, while the chimney looked distinctly cockeyed. Opening the front door of her home, she called out, 'Hey, everyone, come and have a look.' Her mother, Alf, Renée and Ray came to the door. 'Looks a bit suspicious,' they all agreed. 'Better call the police.'

Some moments later a red-haired policeman rode up on a bicycle; the Callows had already placed a wooden and rather whippy ladder against the wall opposite. Cautiously the policeman began to climb, rung by rung, while Ray and Melve held the ladder. He kept climbing while the ladder swayed, and once nearly fell backward on top of Ray and Melve, who were struggling to hold it in place. At last he reached the top rung. Gripping it firmly, he leaned forward, balancing precariously, and looked down through the hole in the roof. What he saw so terrified him that he nearly toppled off the ladder. While Ray and Melve below still fought bravely to keep it in place he managed to draw his whistle and blow a long blast. Then, the whistle clenched between his teeth, he began a hurried, ungainly descent, whistling all the time as strenuously as his lungs would allow. As he neared the ground the Callows demanded 'What's up, officer?' 'A land-mine, a land-mine!' gasped the breathless bobby. Inside the house a two-ton land-mine was hanging on the end of its grey-green parachute, which had been snagged up on a broken beam.

At that moment the Callows' guest, awakened by the shrill blasts of the police whistle and cries of 'Land-mine!' appeared clad only in underpants and vest and carrying in his arms the rest of his clothes, his shoes, bowler hat and attaché case. In this disorderly négligé he bolted down Helen Street, swerved round the corner and was never seen again.

Meanwhile wardens and police came running: five pumps arrived — and so did Mr Callow, back from his week's sick leave. A policeman stopped him in front of No. 1. 'Sorry, guv'nor, no one's allowed to pass; we're evacuating the area.' 'Yes, but that's my bloomin' home!' remonstrated Mr Callow without the slightest effect. His wife and children and scores of others living within 500 yards or so were already being hustled away, carrying a few belongings, by wardens and police. The Callow family, Mr Callow included, camped that night in the Town Hall.

The 15th of September dawned misty over southern England, but soon cleared. On the other side of the Channel Göring's bombers and fighters were arrayed for his triumphal day. It would be a walkover, with only 50 Spitfires left. So, let the battle commence!

It did, around 11 a.m. German tactics were a repeat of those on the 7th; hordes of bombers in massed formation and escorted by fighters bore down on London. The RAF fighters, with ample radar warning and perfect visibility, were able to face them squarely. All day long the German airmen, with dogged courage, came back and back again. But the British fighters, Spitfires and Hurricanes by hundreds, and Ack-Ack were too strong for them. At 6 p.m. that evening Göring, at Cap Gris-Nez, was being told by Kesselring 'We cannot keep it up like this; our losses are rising above the danger line.' The assault was called off. The 'invincible' Luftwaffe had been routed by the RAF fighters whom Kesselring had believed *kaput*. They had downed fifty-six of the Luftwaffe for a loss of twenty-six of their own, with thirteen pilots saved. In Churchill's words, the 15th of September was the 'culminating date' of the day battle. Henceforth it began to turn in favour of Fighter Command.

Not so the night battle — if battle it could be called, at least for the night-fighters and guns, who were yet unable to oppose any serious resistance to the Luftwaffe's unrelenting mass attacks by night on London. Even the indomitable Churchill admitted 'We viewed with stern and tranquil gaze the idea of going down fighting amid the ruins of Whitehall.' The King himself, one of the best shots in the land, kept in practice at his makeshift shooting range in the gardens of Buckingham Palace.

It was on the RAF's victorious day, the 15th of September, as the sirens shrieked a warning for the second time of another enemy attack, that I left Croydon Hospital. Having graduated from crutches to a stick and one leg, I set off to say hullo to my mother in Sussex; it was months since I had seen her, and months more since she had seen her two other sons — Michael, a destroyer captain, and Philip, commanding a battalion of Gurkhas in Burma. The courage of mothers, wives and sweethearts, of a different sort to that of their loved ones, was every bit as fine, and may well have demanded more of them than of their men in the thick of the fight.

My mother was glad to see me. We dined simply, exchanging our news. Michael's ship, she told me, was at Southampton. Next evening I hobbled up the gangway of the destroyer *Viscount*. After dark we cast off, and all night long, with the ships of his flotilla, we scoured the Channel for signs of the invaders.

We need not have worried. Hitler's order, promised for the 17th, was received by his Supreme Headquarters in the early hours of that day while we were still at sea. *Wird Bis Auf Weiteres Verschoben*. Five words which confirmed the postponement of invasion until further notice.

12

TERROR IN THE NIGHT

Despite his gloomy forebodings about the ultimate fate of London, Churchill was more immediately preoccupied with the diverse ways of avoiding such a catastrophe — for if London gave in it would spell the end of British resistance. He kept a close eye on the production of scientific devices, notably special radar for fighters, guns and searchlights. A small number would soon be ready, as would the first of a purpose-built night-fighter, the Beaufighter. He encouraged the development of other devices, strange figments of the inventive boffins' imagination, but which, he thought, were worth a try in the hope of stiffening the feeble night defences. He protested at the hours of work squandered by men and women in factories and offices, obliged by the regulations to take to the shelters. He directed that they should remain steadfastly at their posts until warned by the roof-watchers — nicknamed 'Jim Crows' — that the enemy was overhead. The new system saved millions of working hours and gave workers and officials a proud place in the front line alongside the civil defence.

Churchill worried incessantly about other, more insidious problems which could bring about the downfall of London. He personally investigated them, suggesting his own remedies. One was that of the drains and sewers which had been smashed by the bombing, and threatened the city's water-supply. Another was public health. Night after long night, cramped in the cold and damp of their corrugated-iron Anderson shelters in the garden, millions of Londoners were exposed to the risk of colds, 'flu and other more serious epidemics. One of the Luftwaffe's vain boasts was that they would smash every window in London, with the blast of their bombs. They reasoned with some naïveté that buildings would thus be rendered uninhabitable, and consequently fall into rot and decay. They had made some progress; there was now a glass-famine in Britain.

But in the end, as Churchill said, everything was mastered. Drains and sewers were disinfected and repaired, and the city's water-supply saved. Londoners, gradually inured to the hardships and privations of the 'Blitz', grew resistant to disease and exposure. Gaping windows were made air-tight with sheets of reinforced plastic. If the bombing destroyed many, if not all, of the possessions of thousands of Londoners, it never diminished their heart or their will to resist, nor did it damp their irrepressible sense of humour. Heart, will and humour; these were the arms with which Londoners would defeat the Luftwaffe. And this with but scant refuge from the bombardment; only a very few bomb-proof shelters existed, and available sleeping-space on the platforms of the Underground stations was limited. The great majority of Londoners slept, like the Callows, in their house or in the garden, beneath their Anderson shelter, which was blast-proof — that was all.

Delayed-action (DA) and unexploded bombs (UXB) increasingly menaced London's life. They would paralyse a city district, block the entry to a factory or railway terminus, arrest the traffic on roads and railway lines — until they were dug out and defused. The men of the Bomb Disposal Units, with supreme courage and consummate skill, took charge of this highly dangerous and delicate job. Yet there was no lack of volunteers. One of them, as Churchill recalls, was the Earl of Suffolk, who enlisted his lady secretary and elderly chauffeur to create his private unit. They became known as the Holy Trinity. 'With urbane and smiling efficiency', remarked Churchill, they defused thirty-four bombs. The thirty-fifth sent the Holy Trinity heavenward, where, Churchill continues, he felt sure 'that all the trumpets sounded for them on the other side'. It was not long before the heroic Bomb Disposal Units mastered the DAs and UXBs.

Unexploded 'land-mines' (sea-mines attached to a parachute) were tackled by them with equal valour and skill. Land-mines, like the one which had it exploded would have blown the Callows (and their guest) into eternity, were the ultimate in indiscriminate terrorism against the civilian population. Bombs could be aimed, and usually were, with a precision bomb-sight against military targets. Though they often missed, the will to hit the target was there. But 'this hellish invention', as Churchill had called it years before, of aerial bombardment was rapidly degrading men — young men, decent and brave and good in themselves — into callous murderers of innocent people. The land-mine as a weapon represented the first step in the wilful, wholesale massacre of civilians. It is impossible to aim a land-mine. It drifts down, carried here and there by the wind currents, striking where chance may decide.

Churchill's first impulse was to retaliate, quite simply, land-mine for land-mine, on selected German cities. He bowed, however, to the remonstrations (on moral grounds) of his advisers. Two or three years more and moral objections were to be swept to the winds until, after Hiroshima and Nagasaki, decent men and women would rise up in anger against the massacre of innocents.

For the time being Churchill and his air chiefs contented themselves with avenging, within the limits of morality — that is, by aerial strikes on German military targets — the bombed and beleaguered British, and in every way possible assure their ultimate survival. To this end, incidentally, he began to pay attention to the survival of the War Cabinet, himself included. An impregnable administrative citadel had been prepared out at Hampstead Heath, in North London. After their first meeting there, followed by what the prime minister described as a 'vivacious' luncheon, the cabinet decided they would rather be back in Whitehall, in the thick of the action, even if some of the government buildings, including the prime minister's residence at No. 10 Downing Street, were of ancient and somewhat rickety construction. In time the cabinet offices were to be moved to the 'Annexe', at Storey's Gate, not far from No. 10, and proof against direct hits.

Churchill's anxieties were not confined to the Blitz on London. His thoughts went out far beyond our coasts and the continents beyond. He feared for the safety of Malta, the island fortress in the Mediterranean, within easy reach of attack from Italy. He pressed for the reinforcement (by units in Palestine, Kenya and South Africa) of the 30,000-strong British army guarding their stronghold in Egypt, against which an Italian army some quarter of a million strong was already advancing. Churchill was particularly concerned for a Free French force, with General de Gaulle in command, which was at sea heading for Dakar, the Senegalese capital, with the intention of seizing it from the Vichy French, Hitler's allies. Fears for the secrecy of de Gaulle's expedition were already felt. The brave Free French, indiscreetly clad in tropical uniform as they awaited embarkment at Liverpool, were enthusiastically toasting *'Bon voyage à Dakar'*, ignoring those charming little posters in every railway carriage and public place: 'Careless talk costs lives.' Vichy was thus forewarned. (In the issue, the operation was abandoned.)

Of all Churchill's many worries the greatest, inevitably, was for Britain's Atlantic lifeline. Britain's lone stand would be in vain could she not maintain her line of supply, hundreds of ships, sailing in convoy from the ports of her ally Canada and of her good friend America — not yet an ally by the rules of war — bringing food, equipment and munitions to Bristol, Cardiff, Swansea, Liverpool and Glasgow. These were all Britain's most vital ports, now that London was ceaselessly under fire.

The defeat of Britain's ally France had left that ill-fated country's airfields at the free disposal of the Luftwaffe for the close-range bombing of Britain. France's ports provided convenient bases for the Kriegsmarine's U-boats to prey with greater ease on Britain's Atlantic convoys. The U-boats were now inflicting devastating losses on British shipping.

The Royal Navy was short of destroyers. Churchill had been promised fifty more by President Roosevelt in return for the lease of British bases in the West Indies. But despite his repeated pleas to the American president, the delivery of destroyers was lagging, and when they did arrive they needed a lengthy refit.

In all this broad panorama of anxiety, doubt and disaster, one central fact was certain. Hitler in July had decreed the elimination of Britain as a base for continuing the war against Germany. For this very reason Britain had to survive.

13

NIGHT-FIGHTERS

It was with joy that on 22 September I rejoined my squadron at Church Fenton, a grass airfield in Yorkshire. Though I was still on one leg and a stick, that would not prevent me flying. Willing hands bundled me into the cockpit of a Hurricane. I took off and performed a few aerobatics over the airfield. When I reported myself to the medical officer as fit for flying several witnesses were ready to support me. They were not needed; the doctor understood.

Three months of fighting had thinned out the ranks of the battered squadron I had been sent to command in June. Since then we had been battered even harder. Seven pilots, myself included, remained, and we found ourselves doing the same job as we had done in June: teaching pilots fresh from the training schools to be war pilots. British, Poles, Czechs and French came to us. We kept some, to make up our numbers; the others went on to squadrons in the south. The French, François de Labouchère and Émile-François Fayolle — we called him Émile to avoid confusion — stayed. Why, I do not know, in view of what was about to befall us. Their English was barely sufficient to understand the clearest instructions on the R/T. But both were, in the French sense of the word, extremely *sympathique*. We were happy to have them, and they, as it turned out, were glad to be in our midst.

For a month, as teacher or pupil, we all worked conscientiously at our task of war training — formation flying, aerobatics, mock combats and practice shooting — a regular day-fighter routine. We even flew low over Leeds in close squadron formation to inspire people to give to the Spitfire Fund — rather galling for pilots of a Hurricane squadron, but worthwhile, like everything else we were doing. 'Worthwhile', however, was not enough. There was not one of us who did not feel it his duty to be back in the fray, down south where our comrades were still fighting and dying in their fierce and victorious battles against the Luftwaffe's day offensive.

Gradually the Luftwaffe was wilting. On 27 September they took another terrible hiding from the British day-fighters, losing 55 of their aircraft. Such losses, as Kesselring had warned Göring two weeks ago, were more than the Luftwaffe could stand. Now the British were bleeding it white. The following day a dramatic change appeared in the German tactics. Thirty only of their fastest bombers, Ju 88s, escorted by nearly three hundred fighters, advanced cautiously on London, but were repelled. Göring had to admit that his much-vaunted knock-out blow had failed.

The Luftwaffe chief, chastened and depressed, had departed the battlefield for his hunting retreat, the Reichjägerhof, a log-cabin near Rominten in East Prussia. He discarded his garish uniform of a Luftwaffe Reichsmarschall for the more folkloric apparel of a Reichjägermeister: green suede hunting-jacket over a silk blouse with long puffed sleeves, hunting top-boots and a hunting knife slung from his belt. There at the Reichjägerhof, while trying to console himself in his humiliation of having betrayed his Fuehrer with empty promises, he was still dreaming up new and more horrible schemes to crush the cursed British.

On 7 October he declared his new aims for the Luftwaffe: progressive and complete annihilation of London; the paralysing of Britain's war potential and civil life and, through terror and privation, the demoralization of London and the provinces. These congenial tasks he assigned to his night-bombers. On 18 October, in a pep talk to bomber crews, he said, 'You have caused the British world enemy disastrous losses. . . . Your courageous attacks on the heart of the British Empire, London, have reduced British plutocracy to fear and terror.' That last remark, had they heard it, would have given a good laugh to Londoners like the Callows!

On 20 October Göring called a halt to his day-bomber offensive. While costing his Luftwaffe very dearly, it had not fulfilled his dream of conquest. Now that the night offensive was well under way, Göring began to feel better.

On 21 October, Trafalgar Day, I received a signal from Fighter Command: '85 Squadron has been selected to specialise in night fighting forthwith . . .' Some people have used the expression 'relegated to night-fighting'. They would hardly have done so had they first tried out for themselves this difficult and hazardous occupation.

14

GROPING IN THE DARK

I was at first dumbfounded by this unexpected news. While it is always flattering to be 'selected' to do some special job, it had never occurred to me that I should be asked to transform 85 from a seasoned and successful day-fighter squadron into a wholly night-fighter squadron. Not a word was mentioned about any specialized equipment which might aid the process. There was practically nothing about the Hurricane that could remotely qualify it as a true night-fighter. It did, admittedly, possess a headlight mounted in the wing, but this little luxury was more useful on the ground than in the air. The dashboard instruments were luminous, but could not possibly be a pretext for assuming that the Hurricane was fit for a specialized night-fighting role, any more than could the two small adjustable lamps which diffused a sombre orange glow in the cockpit; they helped just a little in reading the compass, already half hidden beneath the dashboard, and might have helped to read a map. But what good was a map when flying in the pitch-darkness of the blackout? The optical gun-sight could be illuminated by the throw of a switch, and always was before going into combat, by day or by night, so there again there were no grounds for claiming it was specially adapted for night-fighting. And on the right-hand side of the cockpit was a Morse key which operated a light beneath the cockpit,

94

practically as invisible to ground observers by night as it was by day.

While the Hurricane was a formidable day-fighter, had operated at night, and would in future do so, it was not designed as a night-fighter and would never perform properly as one. What the Hurricane did *not* possess told even more heavily against its suitability as a night-fighter. First, it was not fitted with a radar set. Had it been possible to install one, there would be need as well for a radar operator. But the Hurricane was a single-seater. Single-engined too, which put it at a high risk in case of engine failure at night. If the 'elastic' broke, there was little for it but to bail out, Moreover, its lusty Merlin engine spouted tongues of flame through kidney-type exhaust ports which (to prevent the pilot being blinded) were ingeniously screened from his sight. They were, however, visible to the enemy from afar.

And again: flying by night throughout the coming winter would expose both pilot and machine to sub-arctic temperatures. The Hurricane's cockpit, so uncomfortably hot in summer that I nearly always flew in shirt-sleeves, became excruciatingly cold high up during the autumn nights. The nights of mid-winter were sure to be torture, for there was too little space, the plane's instruments and levers were too closely grouped, to allow the wearing of bulky flying-suits, boots and thick gloves.

I pondered on all these forbidding thoughts, but it was not long before I felt resolved. Another passing thought for Nelson: it was Trafalgar Day, and 'England expects . . .' My mind dwelt no longer on the terrors of the night. We were after all fighters whose duty it was to defend Britain by night as well as by day. The day battle had been won, but London was still being cruelly and ceaselessly assaulted night after night, and that for the last six weeks. Nor were provincial cities spared. No one, not even Churchill, could possibly tell if, or when, the attacks would cease. He pondered gloomily at that time on the prospect of London being gradually reduced to a rubble heap, yet Londoners continued to treat the bombardment with disdain.

They went about their business as usual, their pleasures too. Pubs, restaurants and theatres were full, and it was always possible to jump on a tram or a bus, or hail a taxi to get you home. Churchill, who during the grim days of the Battle of France had frequently flown to Paris for talks with the government, was happy to see how the spirit of Londoners compared with 'the frightful squawk' which went up from defeatist elements when the first few bombs had fallen upon the French capital.

London was 'taking it', and at heavy cost. But where were we, its appointed guardians, yet incapable of defending its seven million citizens? It was high time we came to their rescue. The bewildering thoughts of leading a specialized night-fighter squadron which might help, as we had helped by day, in the defence of London and the provincial cities no longer assailed me. I now viewed the prospect as a formidable challenge; one which, in any case, could not be refused. But what tribulations lay ahead! On 23 October the Squadron moved to Kirton-in-Lindsey, a grass field (yet another) in Lincolnshire. Ten miles away, at Caistor, we were allotted a spacious meadow as a 'satellite' airfield. Half a dozen of us were well tried in night-flying, though hardly of the 'specialized' type. The rest had yet to be converted and disciplined in this exacting and frustrating sort of warfare.

15

INVISIBLE BEAMS

While all through the long summer days the air battles had raged, the Germans and British were engaged, silently and obscurely, in the 'Wizard War'. After the Dunkirk evacuation in early June, the Germans set to without delay to erect a chain of Knickebein transmitters in northern France; word reached Dr Jones through the underground that a Wotan transmitter — he had not yet any idea what that might be — was going up on the tip of the Cherbourg peninsula. The Knickebein chain extended through Belgium and Holland as far north as Norway, but above all the collaborationist French Vichy government handed their friend Hitler airfields, ports and beam transmitter sites on a platter, thus giving the German conqueror all the additional means he could desire for subduing Britain — France's ally of yesterday. It was hardly credible that Hitler, with all these winning cards in hand, could possibly fail to 'bring the British to their knees' (one of his favourite, and oft-repeated, expressions). Yet while admiring the British people, he had still to discover their peculiar tenacity, never greater than when faced with an invader.

Like the airfields in France, the beam-transmitter sites, were they destined for Knickebein or, like Wotan, for some other electronic device, put the Luftwaffe within point-blank range of Britain. It was thus that during August their bombers, with their easy-to-use Knickebein, were able to range at night across the length and breadth of our country, attacking small targets at will. Apparently it did not occur to them that they were prematurely showing their hand. When the British had once sorted out their own they would find that with their 'Headache', 'Aspirin' and 'Meacons', it was they who held the winning cards.

On 11 August a Luftwaffe bomber unit, Kampfgruppe 100, moved with its thirty or so Heinkel 111s from its base in Germany to Meucon, near Vannes in Brittany; the field possessed only one small hangar and no runways; it had been used pre-war by a private flying club. The men of KGr 100, after fighting hard in the Norwegian campaign (where a number of them were taken prisoner), returned to Germany to re-form and train. After the rigours of Norway those were pleasant days; the sun shone and the water in the nearby lakes was warm. Often they would fly dressed only in swimming shorts and flying-suits. Their move to Vannes excited no particular attention except among the locals, who remained distant but polite towards the first uniformed Germans they had yet encountered — an attitude which was not to last for ever.

KGr 100's Heinkels were now painted black, with a matt distemper which made them less visible at night, especially to searchlight crews. Apart from that they looked like any other Heinkel, except for the three short radio masts projecting from the top of the fuselage and, of course, the unit's badge, a Viking ship, painted on the fore end of the fuselage. On 13 August, as darkness fell at the end of Eagle Day, KGr 100's Heinkels took off on their first raid on England. It was they who scored those remarkable eleven direct hits on the Nuffield factory at Castle Bromwich, near Birmingham.

The expression X-Gerät (X-apparatus) was not unknown to RAF Intelligence. As early as March 1940 it had been pronounced by a Luftwaffe prisoner of war, who told his interrogator that Knickebein was 'something like X-Gerät'. The Y-service too had intercepted German Enigma high-grade cypher signals which, when broken down by the cryptographers were found to mention X-Gerät. But still the intelligence men remained none the wiser — until mid-August, just at the time when KGr 100 began to bomb Britain. It was then that the Y-service picked up some unusual beam signals which at first mystified the experts. Dr Jones had them code-named 'Ruffians'.

During the rest of August the Y-service, listening day and night, heard further references to 'X-Gerät'. What was more, RAF direction-finding (D/F) stations succeeded in pin-pointing the sources of the mysterious signals, one on the Cherbourg peninsula, others in the Pas de Calais. One night early in September specially equipped RAF aircraft went up to sniff out the beams. The Cherbourg beam was found; it was in some ways comparable to Knickebein, which made it a possible navigational aid. But as far as RAF Intelligence knew, the Luftwaffe possessed no radio receiver capable of being tuned to the extra-high frequency of the beam in question. So they assumed for the moment that the baffling signals must be used by the Kriegsmarine for guiding their ships into harbour.

In the Luftwaffe it was fairly common knowledge among air-crews that there did exist a hush-hush unit which no one could name or number, a unit specialized in blind-bombing. RAF Intelligence themselves, vaguely aware of the same rumour, were certain sooner or later to discover the truth. This they eventually did during the interrogation of a KG 53 crew shot down late in August. The German airmen named the specialized unit as KG 100 — most precious information, though erroneous in one respect. Instead of KG — Kampfgeschwader, with a strength of some 100 aircraft — they should have said KGr, Kampfgruppe, a unit some 35 aircraft strong. Small matter (though the error was to persist for some time in British secret documents). With the Luftwaffe unit's number — 100 — Air Intelligence were now hot on the scent, helped by the Y-service. Further indiscretions by captured Luftwaffe aircrew during interrogation or as they chatted to one another — unaware that the British were eavesdropping with hidden microphones — gave away more secrets.

By the end of September Dr Jones had fitted together enough pieces of the puzzle for Professor Lindemann to inform the prime minister: 'The Germans are making great efforts to improve the accuracy of their night-bombing.' He mentioned that the new beams had been detected, and went on: 'One Kampfgeschwader, KG 100, consisting of about forty machines, has been equipped with special new apparatus to exploit the beams' which, he believed would enable them to put down their bombs within twenty yards of the target. Here he exaggerated somewhat. Their accuracy in practice was more like 120 yards, but such marksmanship was deadly enough.

The 'Prof' also confirmed: 'We know the exact location of the sources of the beams in question.' This being so, he suggested three possible means of defence against the new bombing menace. Either the enemy bombers might be destroyed on the ground by the RAF bombing Vannes or the beam transmitters might be knocked out by aerial bombing or commando attack. Or, finally, the beams themselves could be neutralized by radio jamming.

The latter method, in which the RAF were becoming expert, was the one chosen. Dr Cockburn, of the Telecommunications Research Centre at Swanage, was immediately summoned to produce a suitable jammer. But as in the case of Knickebein, no such ready-made apparatus existed, so the ingenious doctor borrowed an army radio set and modified it, giving it the code-name 'Bromide'. Like 'Aspirin', the special Knickebein jammers, 'Bromide' could not be manufactured overnight in sufficient numbers. Many, many nights of Luftwaffe raids were to pass while Cockburn and his team toiled away to meet the demand. In the interval KGr 100, the suspected villains, continued with impunity and precision to 'mark' with medium-weight explosive bombs the selected target, the upward-leaping flames from which formed a beacon for the rest of the attacking bombers, navigating with less accurate Knickebein. Sometimes KGr 100, instead of marking targets for mass raids, attacked on their own some isolated target, unaware that on each occasion they were imprinting their own particular trademark on the target. Dr Jones's intelligence sleuths, true to the Sherlock Holmes tradition, were quick to discover that when the line of craters left by the 'stick' of German bombs was prolonged southward on a map it invariably led back to the X-Gerät directional beam transmitter on the Cherbourg peninsula. Elementary, my dear Jones!

Knickebein was beginning to run into trouble. At first the Luftwaffe crews had been excited by their new and simple navigational aid, but they very soon had the uncomfortable feeling that the British were fiddling with it. To begin with, when only 'Headache', the collection of modified diathermy and Lorenz sets, was at work, the jamming though fairly weak was enough to give disconcerting proof to the Germans that the enemy had rumbled their Knickebein; that he knew exactly the target for which the bombers were heading, and could warn the defending night-fighters and AA guns accordingly. Considering the shortcomings of our night defences, the effect of 'Headache' was rather more psychological than practical. But it was a good start to the jamming offensive, soon to be reinforced by 'Aspirin'.

'Aspirin' was ready to join the invisible defence just as the night blitz against London began in early September. Its dots and dashes, disagreeing with those of Knickebein, put confusion among the German bombers, sending some of them literally flying round in circles or ending up lost in the pitch-dark. The 'Meacons', false radio beacons planted by the British, added to the havoc played with the enemy's radio-navigation system. Even KGr 100, so far immune to jamming as it approached the target, was not spared as it tuned in to its radio beacons on the way back to base. One of its Heinkels returning to Vannes after a raid on Birmingham in late August was caught out by one of the phoney beacons, situated at Templecombe in Somerset. The *beobachter* (observer), Feldwebel Hilmar Schmidt, was certain they were homing on the beacon at Brest, south of Vannes, when he became muddled by a series of bearings so misleading that he yelled over the intercom, 'Christ, we're not flying backward, are we?' When searchlights held their Heinkel, Schmidt called to the *flugfuehrer* (pilot) Knier, 'I think we're over England!' Knier then turned on to a south-easterly course which, God willing, would lead them to hit the French coast somewhere. When at last they landed, bewildered and exhausted, it was at Berck, near Boulogne, about 250 miles from their base at Vannes!

By the end of September KGr 100 had their eye in; they had made some forty attacks on Britain, half of them on London, the rest on industrial targets; if near misses were more frequent than direct hits, the exceptional precision of their bombing, compared with that of other units, was evident. In October the usual load of high-explosive bombs carried in KGr 100's Heinkels was replaced by a full load of incendiaries, packed into containers which opened automatically as they fell, scattering their fire-lighting devices. Considering KGr 100's prowess in precision bombing, it was surprising that they should switch to such a non-precision weapon. But the precision, however diminished, would prove adequate, and the reason for the incendiaries was soon made clear. In the meantime RAF Intelligence had enough evidence, both from hearsay and from that culled from the air by the Wireless Intelligence (Y-service), to link KG 100 (as the British still called the unit) directly with X-Gerät. Tangible evidence which would reveal the whole system and its possibilities was still lacking. The British would have to wait a little longer.

16

BOMBERS' MOON

Autumn was fading into winter. Since the first week in September, when the blitz started, the city had been raided every single night by an average of over 150 bombers, and often by day too. People were now beginning to find the deadly routine almost monotonous: sirens would begin wailing just as in the failing light workers left the office or shop to queue patiently (and perhaps a little fearfully) in the damp cold for the next bus or tube train. Home at last and weary, they would sit down to a dull and meagre supper, then automatically go off to the shelter if so minded, and if not (like the majority) straight to bed. Sleeping fitfully through the night bombardment, they could rely on the All Clear to wake them around six o'clock next morning. Then, after a quick breakfast of tasteless 'national' bread, sparingly spread with butter or, failing that, margarine and washed down with a cup or two of tea they would be off soon after 7 a.m. for another day's grind. Yet Londoners seldom failed to find something to laugh about in their dreary daily round.

At No. 1 Helen Street, Woolwich, all the Callow family went off cheerfully every day to work. The old man was back at his job in the big-gun shop, now temporarily repaired. The day over, he would pay his customary visit to the Little Bull, where he would stand chatting with his mates and sinking pint after pint until closing-time. Nothing on earth, and least of all in the dark heavens, could intimidate either publicans or their patrons; opening and closing times were faithfully respected. Mrs Callow — the old girl, as her husband called her — seldom went out, but did sometimes accompany her husband on Saturday nights to the local. For this good lady a visit to the Little Bull was as good as going to Buckingham Palace and she dressed up in her finery for the occasion. One port and lemon, or at the very most two, would last her the whole evening.

It was during a heavy raid one night in mid-October when the moon was full that the door of the Little Bull was flung open and there stood a man, panting and shouting: 'Heard the terrible news?' While he caught his breath the startled patrons were expecting at least to hear that the Germans had landed or the prime minister was dead; then the man spluttered: 'The Eagle's been hit!' A groan went up from the patrons of the Little Bull; the Eagle was another of the favourite pubs. The news was bad enough, but sadly worse was to come: many of the Eagle's patrons had that night drunk their last pint on this earth.

Cinemas too never closed. Renée, Ray's youngest sister, was on duty as usherette at the Granada every day. When the sirens went a polite warning was flashed on the screen. 'If patrons wish to leave, they are invited to do so.' Few did. At the Arsenal, vital target as it was for the Luftwaffe, the workers (Ray's sisters Amy and Rose and Kathleen, Johnny's wife, among them) were now so used to the sirens — the 'moaning minnies' — that they only left their work for the shelters if the raid was signalled overhead. Mercifully, of the scores of bombs which fell on the Arsenal, none scored a bulls-eye on the Danger Buildings, where Kathleen was sewing up bags of cordite. Kathleen was at work by eight o'clock every morning. Back home at 7 p.m., her day was not yet finished. Kathy spent two out of three nights alone, while Johnny was on duty at the fire-station. Throughout the night, as an air-raid warden, she stood by, sleeping fully clothed, waiting for a possible telephone call. When it came she reported a few minutes later to the air-raid post. Next morning, around seven, she was off again to work in the Arsenal.

Young Ray too was busy day and night, though at his school, Burrage Grove, where the ground floor had been taken over by the AFS as a substation, a shortage of teachers meant less work and more play — fun while it lasted, but Ray would later have to make good his neglected education. His day began with football, but when after their night's battle with the flames the firemen returned their equipment was washed down on the playground. That put an end to football, and there began a long session in the classroom, where — at least for Ray, bent over his aircraft models — the hours passed quickly. Back home at the end of the afternoon, the serious work began. As the family shopper he ran (literally) errands for his mother, buying the few household necessaries she could afford and food, in return for ration coupons. At the same time he scrounged firewood to keep the single home fire burning. Ray ran everywhere; it was the best way of keeping warm, now that winter was round the corner. He and the gang had invented their patent hand-warmer — a 50-cigarette tin pierced with a few holes and filled with smoking embers. They whirled it round on the end of a length of string. The embers glowed, heating the tin, which they clasped with their frozen hands.

Every evening, in Scout's uniform and tin hat, he ran down to the Town Hall to report for duty to his troop leader. From the basement, which could shelter two hundred, the incessant demand for tea kept Ray busy. But working outside appealed far more to his adventurous spirit. No matter if the bombs kept raining down, he kept running, alone, taking messages from the shelter marshals, carrying bags full of fish and chips to the hungry wardens. Around midnight he ran back home and then, as he would say in his Londoner's rhyming slang, it was up 'the apples and pears' — the stairs — through the 'Rory O'More' — the door — and into 'Uncle Ned' — bed — tired and happy at having done his bit for his country.

On Sundays he would put on his 'whistle and flute' — his suit — and go for a 'ball of chalk' — a walk — which nearly always took him up to his brother Bert's balloon site on Woolwich Common. He was never without a bucket as he walked, for Ray and his gang vied with each other in collecting shrapnel — shell and bomb splinters. The nose-cap of an AA shell was their most coveted find.

Early in October one of Bert's balloons came under enemy fire when a German plane dived down out of the night, its guns blazing. Holed by bullets, the grey, unwieldy monster began to deflate and sink earthward. It flopped down in the middle of Woolwich, its wire cable, nearly a mile long, wrapping itself round houses and a tramcar. Firemen took many hours to unravel the tangle.

The embarrassment caused by Bert's balloon was, at least for the firemen, a minor incident compared with the perils of fire-fighting. During these ceaseless nights of bombardment Johnny and his comrades, armed only with hoses, yielded not an inch of ground in their private war against the Luftwaffe. One of their fiercest battles was fought at the Rotherhithe oil refinery, on the U-bend of the Thames. Johnny's No. 2, Fred Cosh, was at the wheel as they sped down Evelyne Street, where his parents kept a café. Fred's first thoughts were for them. 'Hope the bleedin' cafe's not burning,' he murmured feelingly. It was not, but houses near by were going up in flames. These were personal tragedies, destroying the cherished belongings and often the lives of the occupants.

Rotherhithe oil-refinery was another affair, a monstrous impersonal conflagration. One of the huge, shiny cylindrical oil-tanks had become a volcano of belching fire and dense black smoke. Pierced by bomb splinters, it spewed forth hot crude oil, greenish in colour, which fed the encircling flames and seeped farther afield, forming a slimy, evil-smelling lake. The firemen waded into it in order to play their cooling jets of water on to another tank and prevent it exploding. As they advanced nearly waist-high in oil they could feel it oozing over the top of their high boots, filling them from the feet upward, then creeping up their thighs till it soaked through to their underpants. At least at that depth the surrounding oil helped to support them. As it dispersed and the level fell they began to slither and flounder in the foul green sludge. Occasionally one of them slipped and fell flat and his mates, laughing, helped him up again, daubed from head to foot in the smeary, viscous mess. Thus Johnny and his team, with dozens of other firemen, fought on for twelve hours through the night until dawn, when relief came at last. It was not before next evening that the blaze was extinguished, the battle won.

Towards mid-October the moon, to the Luftwaffe's relief, was waxing. Bombing in the pitch dark held no appeal for them. They had been trained to perfection to bomb by day, and this they did during the Battle of France, though frequently attacking towns without the slightest concern for the civilian population. The devastation and terror they caused earned them the name of 'the invincible Luftwaffe', but the Battle of Britain robbed them of that enviable title. Their losses were far heavier than the RAF's — every aircrew knew it, and realized too that such losses could no longer be sustained. The Luftwaffe bombers were thus driven to attack under cover of darkness — a lesson that RAF Bomber Command, following their own appalling losses during daylight raids, had more quickly understood. With their traditional practice of D/R (dead reckoning) navigation RAF crews more often than not managed to pin-point their targets at night, though they did not always hit them.

When the bombers of the Luftwaffe were attacking British targets by day they generally obeyed strict orders not to bomb unless the target was clearly visible; when it was not they returned to base with their bomb-load. Identifying a target in daylight was one thing; at night it posed a far more serious problem, and the Luftwaffe's system of radio beam navigation and the automatic release of the bombs did not require any precise pin-pointing of the target. Certainly there were conscientious aircrews who tried, but in the darkness all too often failed.

With such inhibitions the Luftwaffe men soon began to feel that there was little profit in night-bombing, though this did not deter them in the least from scattering high-explosive and incendiary bombs all over London. Those crews who fell into British hands tried to justify themselves by claiming that they had aimed at searchlight and AA sites. Crews who were known to have dropped land-mines — which, impossible to aim accurately, were the ultimate in indiscriminate attack on the civil population — would not admit to it, though they agreed that these weapons were being used. One Luftwaffe man remarked that land-mines were after all just the thing for blasting small houses into ruins. Others like him betrayed the same streak of sadism — as indeed did some of our own bomber aircrews, like the distinguished pilot (a man of dauntless courage) who harangued me one day with the need to 'give it 'em back'. 'We must bomb the lot, men, women and children.' Not all bomber crews were so inhuman. Their chief concern was to hit the target. When one Luftwaffe bomb-aimer was told that his bombs had fallen on workers' houses, and had killed women and children, he broke down and sobbed, 'I'm sorry; it's terrible.'

Londoners also cried out to be avenged. When Churchill came among them in the ruins of their homes they cheered him and shouted 'Give it 'em back!' Londoners were 'taking it', and it was hardly surprising that they called out for vengeance against equally innocent and defenceless German civilians. This was total war, fought not by armed men alone but by civilians too. They were in the front line, and as brave as any.

The Luftwaffe were well in their stride in the offensive aimed, in Göring's words, at 'the progressive annihilation of London'. Their bombers were provided with improved equipment: dinghies fitted with automatic SOS radio transmitters and, on some of the Dornier 17s, inflatable bags to keep the aircraft afloat. For the comfort of the crew there was an extra supply of first-aid kits, tins of chocolate dosed with caffeine and special 'Pervertine' pills to sustain them against the rigours following a ditching in the sea. There was also an innovation — special steel helmets for wireless operators, who were apparently more vulnerable than their crew-mates.

The clean lines of many Dorniers and Heinkels were disfigured by a clumsy-looking but effective anti-balloon device — a metal bar extending from each side of the aircraft's nose to the wing-tip, with a cutting edge to sever the cable. However, all this additional paraphernalia (which also included side machine-guns, armour-plating and eventually a fifth crew-man) had to be paid for by reducing the bomb-load, otherwise with the limited take-off run on most Continental airfields, the bomber could not get safely airborne.

The bombs with which the Luftwaffe assailed London were of several types, each with a resounding name: *Splittenbomben* (metal fragmentation), *Betonbomben* (concrete fragmentation), *Sprengbomben* (high explosive), *Minenbomben* (mines) and *Panzersprengenbomben* (armour-piercing). They came in a variety of sizes and again under a bizarre assortment of names: 'Satan', the super-heavy *(uberschwere)* of 1800 kg; Kampf-geschwader 55 were the 'Satan' specialists, bombing with the high-precision Lofte sight from about 20,000 feet. Next came another super-heavy, 'Fritz', weighing 1400 kg. The 'heaviest' *(schwerste)* category included two high-explosive bombs of 1000 kg, 'Esau' and 'Hermann' (a doubtful compliment to Göring). Bombs of 500 kg were labelled 'heavy' *(schwer)*; then followed the lighter weights, 250 kg and 50 kg. Every one of them hellish weapons in their particular way, they brought death and lasting injury to tens of thousands of British civilians. Yet those which in the end were to prove the more devastating were the *Flammen-bomben* (literally 'flame-bombs') and *Brandbomben* (fire-bombs or incendiaries). The Flam 500 and Flam 250, filled with oil (the British called them oil-bombs), sent up a huge mushroom flame on impact. The *Brandbomben*, each weighing a kilogram, were packed, thirty-six at a time, in containers which as they fell opened automatically, scattering their fire-raising contents.

Such then were the arms and the men pitted against the people of London, and later her sister-cities in the provinces, in the implacable war in the dark.

Another arm had for some time been the subject of talk among the Luftwaffe — gas. Rumours had been circulating for some time that the British had used gas shells at Dunkirk, and that a Whitley bomber forced down at Oldenfield in Germany was loaded with canisters containing 'microbes'. Although these rumours were entirely groundless, it was true that the British were well prepared against gas warfare. As young Ray had experienced, the risk of gas had been ceaselessly drummed into the public, young and old. Wardens lectured Ray and his fellow-pupils at Burrage Grove School on the subject. Every British citizen possessed a gas-mask. Johnny and his friends invariably carried theirs wherever they went, as we did in the armed forces. I myself had been on a gas course and learnt how to identify, by smell or otherwise, the various types of gas. I had been made to wear gas-proof clothing — 'goon-skins' — and had stood with a group on Salisbury Plain while an aircraft flew overhead and sprayed us with a reddish liquid which, had it been the real thing, and had we not had our goon-skins and masks, would have blistered our skin, congested our lungs and finally left us dying in agony.

Although the frightful eventuality of gas warfare had not yet materialized, it was never far from the minds of Luftwaffe aircrews. They were firmly convinced, however, that Germany would not be the first to use gas. The Fuehrer, they recalled, was an old infantryman, he was 'kind and humane' and so, they thought, would never employ such a fiendish weapon. But if the British were to employ it first Germany would retaliate with both gas and germ warfare. And Britain, the theory went, being small and overcrowded, would be at a disadvantage.

As the war, to Hitler's dismay, dragged on into October their attitude began to change. If things came to a stalemate it was possible that Germany might attempt to force a decision by using gas — the lethal kind, or perhaps *Nervengas*, which had a stupefying effect lasting six hours or so. If, on the other hand, the British became desperate it was they who might be the first to resort to gas warfare, in which case Hitler (kind and humane as he was thought to be) would order immediate reprisals. In any case, the German public, whose gas-mask filters had not been renewed since the outbreak of war, were now being prepared for the worst. The Luftwaffe too were ready, with 50 kg gas bombs, and trials had been held at Neustadt with low-flying Dornier 17s spraying gas.

There were not a few Luftwaffe men who during the months-long air offensive to subdue Britain had 'outflown' themselves, were worn down to nervous wrecks or suffering from tummy trouble and various other disorders. They were sent off to sanitoria in Germany for treatment. But the men now flying against London were in good shape, despite their doubts about night-bombing. The euphoria generated by the promise of invasion and a quick victory had passed. Now they were more philosophical. The war against Britain was not going to be easy, but their confidence in the Fuehrer remained undiminished. Invasion, if not for now, would certainly be for spring 1941. In the meantime the war of attrition they were themselves waging against Britain would wear down 'that contemptible little island', as some of them called it, and make it easy for the Wehrmacht when they invaded to overrun it in a few weeks.

Luftwaffe airmen showed surprise at the prolonged resistance of Londoners, and wondered whether Berliners, if put to the same ordeal, would ever hold out so long. But they still had little fear of our night defences, although they seemed to be improving. Balloons were a nuisance, and had on occasions proved fatal to German bombers who had ventured too low. British searchlights appeared to be more numerous and powerful than their own, and our AA guns, which unknown to the Germans were now being fitted with radar 'GL' (gun-laying), were unquestionably shooting with greater accuracy. Both searchlights and guns, however, sited as they were in and around London and other great cities, were a help to the Luftwaffe in identifying, if not their precise target, the city where it lay.

Identification of the target was always the bugbear. The Luftwaffe men longed for the bombers' moon when, given good weather, they could find their way round London with ease. In clear moonlight it was simple to follow the Thames — the river itself, or the fog hanging over it. Large parks where there were lakes or ponds were familiar and favourite landmarks, as was St Paul's, especially at sunrise and sunset or under the moon when London's great cathedral cast long, sharply defined shadows. Railway lines too, converging on the main termini, glistened in the moonlight which revealed as if in the daytime such unmistakable landmarks as Buckingham Palace, Trafalgar Square, Hyde Park and the Houses of Parliament.

Now, in this month of October, under the waxing moon, London lay wide open to the Luftwaffe, whose aircrews rejoiced. Towards the middle of the month Londoners began talking of the 'bombers' moon' and told each other, 'We're going to get it heavy tonight.' The enemy bombers made the most of the moonlight period to batter the capital with repeated, well-directed blows. The heaviest raid of all hit London on the 15th, under the full moon. More than 400 aircraft attacked: 430 civilians were killed, and 900 more maimed and mutilated, while all night long the moon shed its gentle light on the massacre. Five main railway termini — Waterloo, Victoria, St Pancras, Marylebone and Broad Steet — were so badly knocked about that traffic had to be diverted for some days. Yet the following morning commuters from the suburbs somehow managed to get into the city for another day's work — late, perhaps, after picking their way through the streets strewn with shattered masonry and the tangle of firemen's hoses. No matter how awful the shambles, the tradition was 'Business as usual.'

The Callow family had some narrow escapes, but their luck held. Incendiaries fell on the house next door to Johnny's. Luckily he was at home, off duty, that night. He rushed in through his neighbour's front door (unlocked, as custom decreed) and up the stairs where an incendiary bomb was spluttering on the floor of a bedroom. He threw a bucket of water at it, but missed. So with his bare hand he picked up the incendiary and hurled it out through the hole it had already made in the roof — a brave act, for a proportion of the Luftwaffe's *Brandbomben* were fitted with an explosive charge. As it was, Johnny got away with burns on his hand. 'All right, old Callow,' his chief, Fire Commander Thompson, told him, 'you needn't report for duty tomorrow.' But Leading Fireman Callow turned up all the same.

Fate played curious tricks; some tragic, others, fortunately, comic. A few nights later Thompson, a fearless and respected leader, was dozing when the alarm went. With a sudden effort he rolled off his bunk and bent over to pull on his boots. The movement dislodged his two false teeth, which he promptly swallowed. Johnny hurried him off to hospital, where next day the denture reappeared from the other end of his digestive tract. Johnny on hearing the news called on his chief. 'Congratulations', he told him with a smile, 'I hear you've had twins.'

In Mr and Mrs Callow's bedroom at No. 1 Helen Street were two beds, a wide one in which the 'old man' slept when off for the night, and a truckle bed beside it, in which the 'old girl' lay beside him. When he was away on night shift she slept in the big bed. And so it happened that one night, while he was away at work, a heavy jagged splinter fell on the house, smashing clean through the roof and tearing a hole in the bed-clothes and mattress of the bed where Mrs Callow usually slept.

Some nights later Mrs Callow's daughter Rose was rudely awakened when a dud AA shell came clattering down the chimney and plopped on to the floor of her bedroom. A lady in a neighbouring street, on the other hand, while sitting out a raid before her empty fire-place, was blown up the chimney by the blast of a near-by land-mine. She emerged bruised but unhurt, and as black as a sweep.

Young Ray too was in luck one night. As he closed the main door of the Town Hall behind him and ran into Wellington Street there came the whistle of a bomb, uncomfortably close. He made to throw himself flat, but the bomb beat him to it, as it exploded not many yards away. The blast bowled him over, landing him in a small heap on the pavement and paralysing the right side of his cheerful young face. Ray, forty-five years later, still suffers.

As the moon waned there came no let-up in the savage, unrelenting monotony of the bombardment — save for a single night, the 3rd of November, when poor weather and pitch dark deterred the Luftwaffe. Then the November moon began to wax, and Londoners once more told each other 'We're going to get it heavy.' No one could tell how much longer London would have to endure. Churchill himself expected the city to be reduced to 'a heap of rubble'. Luftwaffe aircrews themselves felt the 'London run' was becoming a dreary routine. While Unteroffizier Horst

Goetz, a pilot in KGr 100, admired the 'great show' provided by the London AA guns, they seldom scathed any of the unit's aircraft. His own was never touched. Occasionally he caught sight of a night-fighter which apparently never saw his Heinkel. He summed up those ten weeks of ceaseless nightly raids on London as being like running a bus service. A bus service which accounted for the lives of nearly 13,000 Londoners — innocents like the family of seven, parents and five young children, who were all killed by a single bomb in Woolwich one night. But secret signs were coming through to British Intelligence that the Germans had by now realized that, just as they had failed to crush the British fighters, they would never succeed in subduing London. The signs portended a change in Luftwaffe strategy.

17

NIGHT LIFE, NIGHT DEATH

While London fought the Luftwaffe and the other great cities stood firm under occasional attack, Britain's night defences, as Unteroffizier Goetz had noticed, were having but a negligible effect against the Luftwaffe's offensive. During those long nights of London's martyrdom we in 85 Squadron, destined as we were to be a specialized night-fighter unit, could not raise a little finger to help. Our pilots, unaccustomed to flying in the dark, had been zealously training, night after night, to attain the necessary skill and confidence, while the few of us who were already initiated flew regular but futile night patrols.

Since our move to Kirton-in-Lindsey on 23 October our night-life had been full with training and patrols, but an occasional diversion brought relief from the incessant routine. Hardly had we arrived when the Secretary of State for Air, Sir Archibald Sinclair, descended upon us, accompanied by the officer commanding No. 12 Group, Air Vice Marshal Leigh-Mallory. 'Archie' Sinclair, leader of the Liberal party, appeared, at least in a sartorial sense, a man of the old school. Despite the cold, clammy air and the mud of Kirton, he wore, as was his invariable habit, a black jacket, striped trousers and spats, starched butterfly collar and bow tie with a black homburg hat to match. With his careful articulation he spoke kindly, congratulating me on the Squadron's fine record (we had yet to establish one as night-fighters). He was deeply interested in our new role, about which we conversed at length. I pleaded with him to give us airborne radar (AI) and suitable aircraft with adequate endurance and armament to ensure successful interception and combat at night. I begged him too that as long as we had to make do with Hurricanes he would see to it that our eight .303 guns were provided with the most effective ammunition. At present they were loaded with an even mixture of 'ball', armour-piercing, tracer and 'De Wilde' — the latter, which made a flash on striking the target, was the most deadly. I argued that since by night our chances of intercepting the enemy (let alone engaging him in combat) were so slender, we needed a high proportion of the most lethal ammunition available — De Wilde. This, said Sir Archibald was unfortunately not possible. The De Wilde factory had been demolished during a raid in September, and supplies of its ammunition were not readily available.

We discussed the possibilities of a radar set for single-seater fighters. In theory it was feasible, but no one believed that in the dark the pilot could unaided concentrate at once on flying his aircraft, listening to the controller's directions and watching the radar cathode tube. So I banished this idea from my mind, but held fast to my request for maximum striking power. The logic was so simple; we were not going to intercept often, so the expenditure of De Wilde would be limited; but when we did chance to intercept we should possess the best possible means of knocking down the enemy. Oddly enough, my argument never got through to the great ones until months later.

Leigh-Mallory was listening carefully. Though not originally a fighter-pilot (he began in Army co-operation) he was always deeply interested in what his fighter-pilots had to say. Douglas Bader, the famous legless pilot, was the most influential, though not the only one, of Leigh-Mallory's soothsayers, and his persuasive views on tactics led to a bitter quarrel between L-M and Keith Park, who commanded No. 11 Group. I had met them both some years before the war started, and admired them both in their different ways. When I had taken over 85 Squadron in June it was in 12 Group under Leigh-Mallory, and I got to know him better. Then we had moved south into 11 Group, where I had more chance of appreciating the great qualities of Park. Now we were back again in 12 Group with L-M. I had a feeling that he had an avuncular interest in me, perhaps because he and his brother George (lost mysteriously near the summit of Mt Everest in 1924) had as kids known my mother when she lived at Hartford Hall in Cheshire.

On the morning following the departure of those eminent gentlemen I was nearly killed by enemy fire — not, I hasten to say, in some heroic combat, but while chatting quietly on the ground at Caistor, our satellite field, with Jim Marshall, one of our flight-commanders. He was a likeable fellow, about twenty-two, tall, thin and 'smiley'. He seemed to take a pleasure (which I shared) in teasing me, keeping me always just within the limits of respect for me as his boss. I could always count on his loyalty, and valued his advice. He had fought with the Squadron in France.

As we chatted Jim suddenly dived at me, dragging me to the ground with him on top of me. I went down wondering what on earth had incited this apparently unprovoked offence of striking a senior officer when I caught sight of a Heinkel streaking just above the hedge less than a hundred yards away, the rear gunner pouring forth tracer which zipped just above our heads. We quickly recovered from our surprise, jumped to our feet and yelled, 'Start up!' I could move as fast as anyone on one leg and a stick, but before reaching my Hurricane I was dismayed to see the fitter standing on the wing holding part of the engine cowling in his hand. 'Button her up, quick!' I shouted, but it took him another two minutes. Jim was away well before me. Then I was off, the loose straps of my parachute and fighting harness clacking noisily in the slipstream against the outside of the fuselage until, once airborne, I had time to buckle them up. At 'nought feet' I scoured the local countryside, without result. Jim, however, caught that brave Heinkel and sent it down, but not before it had bombed Kirton, demolishing our squadron offices. Luckily our adjutant, Tim Moloney, and the orderly room staff had gone for lunch. That evening Tim wrote solemnly in the

Squadron diary: '85 has been bombed at Seclin, Merville [in France], Debden, Croydon and Kirton. Total casualties, 1 killed.'

The damp soil of Caistor satellite was soon churned into a quagmire so we returned to Kirton, there to install ourselves permanently and to persevere with the conditioning of our pilots to night-fighting tactics and procedure, where the weather, be it said, was an ever-present menace. Fortunately, those pilots were not yet as aware as the few of us already 'night-operational' of our almost hopeless task, lacking as we did the proper equipment, and above all airborne radar and an effective armament. Our morale, notwithstanding, was high and received a little extra boost when one black night at the end of October Sammy Allard (more by luck than by his own or the controller's judgment) intercepted an enemy aircraft. Not that this fluke was any reflection on his skill. A good-humoured Yorkshireman with a fine head of flaxen hair and a ready if slightly mocking smile, he was another veteran of the Battle of France. As a pilot, by day or by night, he had no equal in the Squadron.

Sammy, patrolling unconcernedly, suddenly saw tracer, from an invisible source, piercing the darkness. He then sighted the navigation lights of two aircraft — no doubt our own, for the tracer was flying in their direction. Sammy closed immediately on the source of the tracer, and although he was unable to discern the shape of an aircraft he could clearly see its exhaust flames, upon which he opened fire, only to be blinded by his own tracer and lose sight of his target.

The very next night, as black as the last, Sergeant Geoff Goodman was surprised while on patrol to see tracer flying all around him. Like Allard, he fired back at the point from which it came, but his aggressor made off unseen in the dark.

Yet again, some nights later, Sergeant Berkley had a somewhat different encounter. Berkley, a newcomer to the squadron and not a veteran of the earlier fighting, soon showed his prowess as a pilot. Hardly more than twenty, he was a tall and softly spoken Irishman whose well-trimmed moustache added to his charm. As he patrolled high up under the nearly full

November moon, the blaze of incendiaries attracted his attention. Down he went, hoping to pick out the enemy bomber against the dazzling carpet of light, but it was he, unfortunately, who became the victim of this manœuvre, offering himself as a silhouette to the enemy, who showered him with tracer. And talking of tracer, it must be remembered that for every glowing tracer bullet there were four or five more invisible, ball and armour-piercing, as well as the Luftwaffe's answer to our own De Wilde — 7.92 mm chromium-tipped bullets which exploded on impact.

Although these fleeting incidents marked the very beginning of the process which would transform us into a specialized night-fighter squadron, they did teach us a lesson or two. Young Berkley's attempt to spot the enemy aircraft silhouetted against the fires started by incendiaries was soon to become a regular tactic, when British cities were consumed by fire sent down upon them by Kampfgruppe 100 in their new role of a *Beleuchter-gruppe* — fire-lighters, and incidentally the first Pathfinders.

The other lesson was that of exhaust flames. Those seen by Sammy Allard and Geoff Goodman came almost certainly from the twin Fafnir engines of a Dornier 17Z, now being used by the Luftwaffe as a night-fighter. The defect of this otherwise excellent power unit was its short exhaust pipes, the flames from which could easily be seen. It was the same problem with our Hurricanes, but the time had come at last to change the exhaust system. We flew our Hurricanes to the Rolls-Royce works at Hucknall, near Nottingham, where in little more than the twinkling of an eye the company's fitters removed the old 'kidney-type', flame-belching exhausts and replaced them with 'stub' exhausts, short and flat, one for each of the twelve cylinders. By cooling and damping the flames they rendered them invisible. In return they gave an exhaust note more deafening than ever, with a racy, staccato crackle when the engine was throttled back for landing. Those were beginner's lessons — more difficult ones were yet to come. Slowly, ever so slowly, we were creeping forward, but a long, dark road still lay ahead.

During these nights my place when not on patrol was on the

flare-path beside the Chance floodlight, connected by field telephone to the operations room and the control tower. A radio set kept me in touch with the pilots navigating tentatively in the dark sky above. Well wrapped against the cold in a sheepskin jacket and wool-lined flying-boots, I could keep a close if blind eye on my men, listen for signs of trouble and transmit messages to them.

It was on a clear moonlight night in November, while the floodlight was illuminated ready for François de Labouchère to come in and land, that another aircraft, invisible but with a decidedly odd exhaust note, flew low overhead. 'Switch off, quickly,' I told the floodlight operator, certain that it was not one of ours. Then to François I called, 'Turn out your navigation lights. Enemy aircraft in the vicinity.' Then I rang the control tower. 'It's O.K.', replied the duty officer, 'it's one of our bombers preparing to land. He's just dropped a message.' At that moment the 'message' exploded — a 50 kg bomb, I should say — and the aircraft was back, machine-gunning vigorously in our direction. The floodlight operator and I both dived under its solid steel chassis. There then followed several moments' acute suspense. François, who had evidently not understood my message, was on his final approach, navigation lights still burning — a sitting duck for the enemy air gunner — while I peered out from beneath the floodlight calling him repeatedly on the radio 'Turn out your lights . . .', but still he did not heed the message. 'We'll have to get out and switch on the light,' I told the operator, and we crawled out into the open. The floodlight threw its beam down the flare-path and the suspense became unbearable. At last François touched down; I gave him a few more seconds to run out after his landing, then 'Out with the light!' I called to the operator.

The enemy aircraft was back, and I could now recognize the silhouette of a Dornier 17, its exhaust flames clearly visible. By some miracle no one inside it had apparently sighted François, who was now taxiing back towards the floodlight, his navigation lights still burning. I threw off my jacket and raced towards him, signalling to him to leave the motor running, jump out and —

tapping frantically on his nearest navigation light — to switch them both off. He understood at last, and a moment later was on the ground beside me. Above the crackle and slipstream of the motor I shouted in his ear 'Give me your helmet and parachute.' Though neither fitted properly I somehow got into them.

At that moment the Dornier came back, very low this time, raking the airfield with machine-gun fire and sending François and me headlong for cover — he beneath the fuselage of the Hurricane and I under the tail-plane, both of which being covered in fabric gave no protection whatever. However, it felt better to be under something, no matter what! Then the Dornier was gone, and a moment later I was up in the cockpit and roaring off the ground in hot pursuit of the intruder. Directed by the controller, I chased him, flat out, eastward into the breaking dawn, but having too much start on me he was gone.

The fun we had that night, if at times somewhat undignified, was all the same exhilarating. It could have been more so had our good friend François had more practice at the game. He had actually sighted the Dornier, closed in behind it and followed it (his navigation lights on) but unsure of its identity he was afraid to open fire. Otherwise, as Tim Moloney noted in the diary: '85's first night victory might have been a Frenchman's.'

On 6 November a signal came in from 12 Group headquarters, ordering the Squadron to move to Gravesend, east of London on the southern bank of the Thames estuary. With it came a personal message from L-M: 'Sorry you are leaving 12 Group again.' That was nice of him.

We were not, however, quite ready to leave. I could not yet declare my outfit 'night operational', because of François and Émile. The language problem was still bugging them, and it was not safe to let them loose in the dark against the enemy. They persevered meanwhile in mastering the patter between pilot and controller. It would not take them long. 85 Squadron was heading in the right direction.

This was far from being the case that morning of 6 November with a Heinkel 111, registered number 6N + BH, of Kampfgruppe 100. It had taken off from Vannes, loaded with six 250 kg HE bombs and two Flam. 250s, to attack Birmingham. At the controls was Feldwebel Hans Lehmann. The rest of the crew were all *feldwebelen* too: Otto Paul, Ludwig Meyerhoffer and Heinz Bitte. They climbed up through solid cloud on a compass course, heading north-east via the Saint-Malo beacon, intending to intercept the directional X-Gerät beam from the Cherbourg peninsula transmitter. But that night they were out of luck. Lehmann soon realized that the gyro (automatic) and magnetic compass readings differed by 90°. Reckoning that he must be somewhere over south-west England, Lehmann let down, hoping to break cloud, find Bristol and unload his bombs on to that vital and historic port. But Bristol was shrouded in cloud. The four *feldwebelen* and their Heinkel were completely lost. Then to his relief the wireless op., Meyerhoffer, obtained a signal which he recognized as the Saint-Malo beacon. Lehmann set course for it on his magnetic compass (which he trusted), and in time received the usual signal indicating that he was overhead. He then altered course for Vannes, 60 miles south, while Meyerhoffer signalled base that they were approaching. Oddly enough, Vannes did not acknowledge, nor was there any sign of the usual searchlight, pointing vertically to indicate the airfield. Down went the Heinkel lower and lower until Lehmann saw that he was over the sea, where he took the precaution of jettisoning his bombs. 'Must be the Bay of Biscay,' he told the others on the intercom. 'We've overshot Vannes.' He turned back northward and soon, in the feeble light of dawn, discerned a coastline. His fuel tanks now nearly empty, Lehmann decided to put down on the first available beach. In the poor light he mistook the breaking surf for shingle, and moments later the Heinkel splashed down into the sea. Lehmann, Meyerhoffer and Bitte managed to get out and scramble ashore. But of Otto Paul there was for the moment no sign.

Beyond the shore stood a rampart of white cliffs. This, they all agreed, was certainly not the Brittany coast near Vannes; they must be in Spain. Two of the *feldwebelen* set off to scale the cliffs while the third stumbled along the shore, hoping to find help. It was soon forthcoming, though not quite as the young German expected. He found himself confronted by a man in khaki, wearing the familiar tin hat of a British Tommy. The crew of 6N + BH had fetched up on the coast near Bridport, in Dorset, duped, as not a few of their comrades had been, by the Templecombe 'Meacon', which they had taken for the beacon at Saint-Malo. The police rounded up the other two, and later in the day the body of Otto Paul was washed ashore. It was buried with military honours, with an RAF contingent in attendance, at the near-by churchyard of Eype.

Technicians from Air Intelligence were on the beach soon after the ditching of the Heinkel. They watched in suspense as the receding tide uncovered the aircraft's markings, 6N + BH, and the emblem of a Viking ship. The Heinkel was unmistakably one of Kampfgruppe 100's, the first to come down in England. But before those keen-eyed detectives could examine the wreck it had first to be salvaged.

This was not as simple as it looked. The Army and the Navy disputed the prize, the Army arguing 'We captured the crew, so the aircraft is ours', the Navy insisting 'The aircraft's in the sea, so it belongs to us'. In the upshot, it was the Navy who towed the Heinkel into deeper water to enable their lifting derricks to approach and haul it out of the waves — which meanwhile had badly damaged the X-Gerät within. But for this foolish inter-Service squabble many inhabitants of the Midlands city of Coventry might have been saved from death.

Air Intelligence meanwhile made another scoop. The Y-service once again picked up some unusual signals which Dr Jones immediately identified as a form of navigational beam. He gave it the code-name of 'Benito', and as usual asked his colleague Dr Cockburn to devise a suitable jamming apparatus. It was to be called 'Domino'. For once Cockburn was not pressed for time; there was no evidence to show that 'Benito' was yet in operation with the Luftwaffe. The Doctor and his team at Swanage were still working feverishly to perfect 'Bromide', the X-Gerät jammer. Unfortunately, they would have to wait for certain vital elements, thanks to the Navy–Army conflict which had committed 6N + BH's X-Gerät to the corrosive influences of the sea.

The November moon was waxing — the bombers' moon again — and Londoners were bracing themselves against another series of mass onslaughts. But the dozen or so enemy aircraft picked up by our coastal radar crossing the Channel early on the night of 14 November were certainly not heading for London, any more than the hundreds of others which a little later came streaming in over the south and east coast. Coventry, not London, was the Luftwaffe's target that night.

Those dozen aircraft in the vanguard were from Vannes. It was KGr 100's job to blaze the trail for the hordes which followed. So clear was the night that the KGr 100 crews, beyond checking their X-Gerät from time to time, hardly needed to use it until the final run-up to the target, upon which they showered, with telling accuracy, thousands of incendiaries. Within an hour the centre of Coventry was blazing so furiously that the following waves of bombers could already discern the conflagration before they crossed the English coast, as a distant pin-point of light, beckoning them on to the slaughter. Ordered to concentrate on aircraft and engine factories, they dealt them many a crippling blow. Yet one entire unit, LG 1, according to the confession of one of its captured aircrews, was ordered to drop their load of bombs not on factories but on working-class districts. The Luftwaffe killed more than 550 Coventry citizens that night, and sorely injured another 800. But neither this fearful massacre nor the demolition of their factories and their splendid cathedral could damp the spirits of the survivors. To the city council's offer to evacuate ten thousand, only three hundred responded. Within a few days Coventry's factories were busy again; such were the exigencies of war. Years were to pass before the city could build a new cathedral.

That night four of 80 Wing's 'Bromide' jammers were in position to foil X-Gerät and the precision bombing it provided for the firelighters of KGr 100. Not one of the jammers was effective, and it was not until the experts of Air Intelligence at last obtained the much-needed clues from the sea-spoiled X-Gerät of the Bridport Heinkel, 6N + BH, that it was found that Bromide was wrongly tuned. A simple adjustment thereupon assured it a highly successful future.

The Luftwaffe's savage assault on Coventry marked the beginning of a new offensive against the British industrial cities. It also signified quite clearly the end of Hitler's dream (and Göring's too) of knocking out London and driving its citizens to mass hysteria and insurrection. But for all that, London remained an envied target. Three nights after Coventry, hundreds of bombers came back for yet another devastating attack on the great city. But the worst, for the time being, was over.

In their paralytic attempt to defend Coventry, and once again London, the night defences — fighters and AA — did little to impede that murderous fire attack. A few night-fighters sighted enemy bombers but failed to bring them down. The AA guns hit one or two. Another bomber collided with a balloon. To these feeble efforts 85 Squadron could make no more than a symbolic contribution. Three or four of us took turns to patrol all through the night. I did a couple of stints of an hour or so, but like the others returned empty-handed.

On the 18th of November I signalled 12 Group 'All pilots night operational.' The following night 85 Squadron nearly lost its commanding officer.

I took off on patrol about two hours after nightfall and climbed up into a sky luminous with stars and the waning moon to 15,000 feet, where I settled down on patrol, guided here and there by the controller. All was quiet in the sector, and nothing disturbed the calm of our brief exchanges: 'Hullo, Wagon Leader, vector [steer] o-one-sixty, angels fifteen [height 15,000 feet]. Over.' 'Wagon Leader o-one-sixty, angels fifteen, over', I acknowledged; thus we chattered while I admired the glory of the heavens. Over an hour had gone by when the controller's voice, this time clearly anxious, sounded in my earphones. 'Wagon Leader, pancake [land] immediately. Low fog is rolling up fast towards the airfield. Hurry. Over.' At that height I had not noticed the fog, but now as I banked the aeroplane and looked down into the dark vault below I saw what looked like a sheet of white, some miles long, unfurling inland from the coast. I put the nose down, and with a vector from the controller, began a long, fast dive towards the airfield. It was going to be a close race.

The fog won; it was more than half-way across the airfield as I swept low overhead and had already blotted out the flare-path. A passing thought struck me: climb up and bale out, but a stronger impulse — 'Get down somehow' — prevailed. I tightened up my harness straps. Wheels down, flaps down and I descended in a left-hand turn, straightening up in line with where I calculated the flare-path must be. The red light on the hangar roof passed just beyond my right wing-tip. It was the last friendly object I saw before plunging into the dense white mass below, where nothing was visible beyond my Hurricane's nose. The rest was going to be delicate, but the wings spread out on each side of me felt as if they were my own; somehow I knew that they would bear me down safely to the ground which could not now be far below.

Peering ahead into the gloom, I waited for the flare-path to show up. Suddenly it was there, glowing faintly, not stretching away in front of me but at 45° to the right of my line of flight. It was too late to turn; I was too low, my airspeed too slow. I could only keep straight on, sightless, into the fog. After throttling back the engine I was conscious of a long, long hush as, carefully feeling the controls, I lowered the aeroplane towards the hidden surface of the airfield, waiting hopefully for my wheels to touch. Before they did the right wing dropped violently — a nasty trick of the Hurricane as it stalled — and the aeroplane dropped out of my hands, crunching into the ground, smashing the under-carriage and careering along for some way before lurching to a stop. My head hit the windscreen, but my harness held the rest of me fast. For a moment I sat there, thanking God briefly but fervently for seeing me through. Then I called the controller, telling him I was down on the airfield but where I could not say. More moments passed until I heard voices and the whirr of engines — the ambulance and fire-tender, no doubt. Calling to them now and again 'Hey-oh! I'm here!' I meanwhile inspected my poor broken Hurricane. The undercarriage was crumpled, the propeller bent and clods of earth had damaged and dirtied the underside of the wings. It might have been so much worse.

The base commander, Stephen Hardy, tall, massive, gentle and ever concerned for the well-being of us pilots, was there. 'Glad to see you alive,' he said. 'I thought you'd bought it.' He drove me to the mess, gave me a beer and, after we had chatted said, 'Now go off to your room and sleep it off.' Unaccustomed to lying between the sheets, I could not sleep — I dressed again and walked back to the pilots' room, where I lay down on a spare bed and pulled a blanket over me. Back in my natural habitat, I soon dozed off.

Tim Moloney, who fussed over us all and faithfully chronicled the Squadron's activities, noted a little stiffly: 'One of the major problems facing the hard-worked adjutant is trying to make his commanding officer get enough sleep.' Tim perhaps had reason to complain, but now that I was so fully engaged in this occult practice of night-fighting, sleep would have to be sacrificed more than ever before. Anyway, I had by now lost the habit.

While that night I patrolled in vain, ending up in a heap on the ground from which I emerged with but a bump on the head, a remarkable young man in his early twenties, John Cunningham, scored a memorable victory. John was a flight lieutenant in No. 604 (County of Middlesex) squadron. He was one of the most skilful pilots in the RAF: there was no reason to doubt it. But with his cherubic countenance — rosy cheeks, fair curling hair and engaging smile — it was hardly thinkable that he had also the makings of a redoubtable night-fighter pilot and a scourge to the enemy. His prowess was to become legendary.

John's victory that night was a near-classic, a model for the future. His aircraft was a purpose-built night-fighter, the first to be built — a twin-engined Beaufighter, fitted with Mark IV AI, the latest in airborne radar, and armed with a formidable battery of four 20 mm cannons and six .303 machine-guns. The one missing element, indispensable to a fully classic combat, was GCI, ground-controlled interception; that is, inland tracking by radar. (The coastal radar chain, effective as it was, could only 'see' outward, over the sea.) Failing GCI, it was the searchlights which helped to direct John on to his target. Spotting a searchlight cone some distance away, he made towards it. His radar operator, Sergeant Phillipson, 'flashed his weapon' — a code expression which, apart from its connotation for the vulgar-minded, meant 'switched on his radar set'. Phillipson, his eyes riveted on the cathode tube, soon obtained a clear, firm 'blip', the tiny shadow which betrayed the presence of an invisible enemy aircraft.

The chase was on, with the radar operator guiding his pilot in behind the enemy, until on the intercom John said quietly, 'O.K., I can see it' — a shape in the dark from which there emanated four clusters of twinkling flames, which led John to think that they came from each engine of a four-engined bomber. With his thumb he pressed the firing button on the control column; the terrible salvo from the Beaufighter's cannnons and machine-guns blinded him. When he ceased firing he could see no further sign of the enemy. Twenty minutes later a Junkers 88, the only hostile bomber down that night, crashed in flames near Selsey Bill in Sussex. Its crew had baled out; they confirmed that they had been shot down by a night-fighter. John's only error, a minor one, had been to mistake the exhausts — two to each of the Junkers 88's twin motors — for those of a four-engined aircraft. 'Exhaust patterns', when we had learnt to identify them, were to be a help in aircraft recognition.

85 Squadron was at last on the move, southward to Gravesend on the outskirts of London. On the way there I stopped off at Debden, our earliest haunt, where we were taking over some of the Hurricanes of 73 Squadron, itself on its way to the North African front. Those aircraft, and the ones we already possessed, were being given (somewhat tardily) a new look — daubed with a lustreless black paint which robbed them of much of their pristine allure and left them with the guileful, sombre countenance of a hunter who stalks his prey in the dark.

It was 22 November, and incidentally my twenty-sixth birthday, which I celebrated with a few friends that evening at the

LONDON ON FIRE

Firemen battle against the flames caused by high explosive and incendiary bombs, 1940-41. In one concerted attack on 29 December 1940 fires raged all night and a quarter of the City (the square mile round St Paul's) was destroyed.

above: Perhaps the most famous wartime picture of St Paul's, ringed by flames. *Daily Mail*

below: No. 23 Queen Victoria Street, London EC4, collapsing in flames. *Guildhall Library*

Above: General view of Ludgate Hill, EC4 (with St Paul's in the background) showing firemen playing hoses on the burnt-out buildings, 12 May 1941. *BBC Hulton Picture Library*

Below: Firemen damping down smouldering debris in Newgate Street, EC4. *Guildhall Library*

the Home Front, volunteers gave their services to organizations involved in rescue and vage work, among them the Civil Defence, ARP, WVS and Salvation Army. Despite mbed hospitals, medical staff carried on their duties as usual.

Above: A damaged ward at Forest Gate Hospital, Tower Hamlet Road, Essex, 2 October 1940. Fortunately the patients had been moved to a shelter before the bomb fell. *Associated Press*

Left: New-born babies being evacuated from the maternity wing of a bombed south-east London hospital, 16 September 1940. *Associated Press*

Top: Rescuers assist a patient extricated from the ruins of St Matthew's Hospital, Shepherdess Walk, London N1. 9 October 1940. *Associated Press*

Above left: Nurses from the same hospital manage to smile as they salvage bedding. *Associated Press*

Above right: Soldiers help clear the damage resulting from a high explosive bomb on the Bank Underground Station, 11 January 1941. The bomb penetrated the carriageway and exploded in the booking office at 8.05 pm. 57 people were killed, including 1 policeman, and 70 people were injured. January 1941. *BBC Hulton Picture Library*

Above: Digging for survivors off the Strand, WC2, 1940. (On the right is the Savoy Chapel.) *BBC Hulton Picture Library*

Below: Damaged wing of St Thomas's Hospital, London, after an air-raid attack, 16 May 1941. *Associated Press*

Right: Rescuers find a survivor at No. 7 Budge Row, EC4, one of several people brought out alive after an air-raid. *Guildhall Library*

Below: A welcome cup of tea from the Salvation Army for families salvaging furniture from bombed houses in Dulwich. *BBC Hulton Picture Library*

ove: A wounded boy is carried from his home by a rescue-worker after being trapped for
1our in his bedroom following a raid on Ilford, in the suburbs of London. *Associated
ss*

ow: Using oxygen and artificial respiration, rescuers attempt to resuscitate a woman
im of a South East air-raid. She recovered and was taken to hospital. *Associated Press*

One of the last bombs to fall on London in the Second World War was a V-2 rocket which landed on busy Farringdon Market in the City on 8 March 1945. 380 people died. But th another, and no less heroic, story of the war years after the period of this book. *BBC Hulton Picture Library*

White Horse in near-by Saffron Walden. I had the faint impression that I was getting on in age. Officially (though there were notable exceptions) twenty-six was the limit laid down for commanding officers of day-fighter squadrons, twenty-eight for night-fighters. But finally it was not age that counted so much as reflexes and a contempt for fear. I was bent on getting my ex-day-fighter squadron off the ground again and into the night air. We raised our glasses (filled with mild beer) and drank to 85's success.

The following day I flew on to Gravesend, where the Squadron, pilots and ground-crew, was now forgathered in full strength. We were pleased to be thrust into the forefront of the defence, between London and the enemy. But how were we going to acquit ourselves, so inadequately armed for night combat? I dared not envisage the future, but could only pray that our high spirits would see us through. They did, though we had still to endure months of frustration and calamity before we were able to approach the success of John Cunningham and Sergeant Phillipson, in their AI Beaufighter.

18

MOURNFUL NIGHTS AT GRAVESEND

Gravesend. The very name was enough to give one the willies, particularly when we were all trying hard not to think of the ever-present possibility of dying an untidy death, our bodies splattered amid the burning, twisted remains of our aircraft. Our brief sojourn at Gravesend was to be an ordeal, yet there was one agreeable feature. We were lodged far from the airfield; the pilots at Jeskyns Court, a pleasant manor house, the ground crews at a place with the droll name of 'Laughing Water'. While the main reason for this was that there existed little accommodation at the airfield for either man or beast, there was another, connected with our role as specialized night-fighters. It was now recognized that after the night's work ground crews and pilots deserved to sleep far from the thunder of day-flying aircraft.

At the break of day, when we were informed by the controller that the Squadron was 'released', we would return to our quarters for eggs and bacon, then to bed, to sleep for six hours or so. When the brutal awakening came we felt little appetite — we were still drowsy — for the lunch being served to the few daytime men of the administrative staff who were known among ourselves as 'penguins'. Why? Because they had cold feet and couldn't fly. Really, we meant them no wrong, for they included veterans like our beloved Tim Moloney who, aged nineteen in the First World War, had risked his neck, and still sported his air-gunner's single wing above the medal ribbons of that war. Others, of a younger generation and undecorated, were condemned through some defect of eyes or lungs or heart to serve as 'wingless wonders'. They were good men, with few exceptions; it was the latter who occasionally provoked our disparaging epithets — penguins or wingless wonders.

At lunch the conversation, more than food, revived us for the next stage — night air-tests during which we tried out our black, sleuthy-looking Hurricanes; the proper functioning of the engine and radio was naturally of prime importance. By instinct, we were tempted by the thrill of a few aerobatics — a loop perhaps, and a few slow rolls. We resisted, however, for such manœuvres upset the gyro-compass and artificial horizon, knocking them off their supports, their gimbals — another of those strange, romantic words which belong as much to aviation as to *Alice in Wonderland*.

> 'Twas brillig, and the slithy toves
> Did gyre and gimble in the wabe . . .

Towards sunset we came to 'readiness', the start of a twelve-hour period of alert spent in a Nissen hut, with its hemispherical corrugated iron roof and concrete floor, upon which were aligned a number of iron bedsteads furnished with a thin mattress and a couple of rough blankets. Though it mattered little to me upon which bed I lay, some pilots were more possessive. One night I noticed a bed with a parachute lying on it and a notice warning 'Hemingway, his bed'. Paddy Hemingway, quietly spoken with a thin moustache that suited him well, was another veteran of the Battle of France, and a close friend of Jim Marshall. An excellent pilot, he showed a remarkable aptitude for being shot down, baling out, and walking or swimming away intact. So far he had a preference for water. Fished out *in extremis* from the North Sea during the Battle of Britain, he jumped down again a few days later into Pitsea Marshes. His career as an involuntary parachutist was not yet ended. Meanwhile his parachute lay there, stating a claim to 'his' bed.

We were summoned, one by one, to the Air Ministry medical establishment for eye tests. It was then that I met a charming man, Air Commodore Livingstone, an ophthalmologist, who explained to me the mysteries of night vision, quite a different optical process to seeing by day. From him I gathered that when you walk out of a lighted atmosphere strange things happen to your eyes. The 'rods' are slowly flooded by a liquid, visual purple, until after about fifteen minutes your eyes are capable of piercing the darkness. The process resulted in 'visual acuity'. Some had it, others did not. I responded satisfactorily to the tests of Dr Livingstone, who then began talking about contact lenses. They were something new. Though I had no need of them myself, the doctor told me that he knew several pilots, bombers mostly, who had faced the flak of Berlin and the Ruhr without a qualm, but who cried out in agony at his attempts to fit them with contact lenses. Each one of us has his own kind of courage. It was henceforth ordained that pilots awaiting their turn to patrol must wear dark glasses so that their eyes might already be adapted to night vision before take-off. This did not discomfit us in the least, for our Nissen hut was permanently illuminated by the glaring light of a number of kerosene lamps. They burnt with a small but disturbing roar which denied us the opportunity of dozing, let alone sleeping, however lightly.

Outside our Nissen hut our swarthy Hurricanes waited, like tethered horses. Since we parted singly on patrol, a 'scramble' (take-off) at night was a less hurried affair than by day. It was as well, for the surface of Gravesend airfield was plastered with a thick layer of mud through which, after discarding our black glasses, we had to plod in order to mount our own personal charger. Then, right foot in the stirrup (a retractable step) which scraped off its small share of mud. Left foot, then right, on to the wing where you left your slimy footprints and finally, swing the right leg over into the cockpit and on to the seat — the mud deposited there rubbed off eventually on your bottom. Once in the cockpit — your night vision, thanks to the black glasses, perfectly adapted — the engine-fitter helped to strap you in, shining his torch on the quick-release fastenings, the instrument panel and, inevitably, straight into your eyes, whose carefully nurtured night acuity would vanish in an instant.

The nicety of pre-adapting your eyes to night vision, while appreciable, was not all that important. Once the pilot was in his cockpit, and set for take-off he had but to peer forward along the long nose of his Hurricane and point it into the dark sky. Soon after take-off the eyes became transformed so that they could see like those of a cat.

The mud problem, however, persisted. What had been scraped off on the rudder-bar and the cockpit floor gradually dried out into dust which on opening the cockpit hood was blown by the slipstream into your eyes. The coating of mud remaining on your boots eventually froze solid when you reached the sub-zero temperature of your patrol altitude.

That was the personal side of the mud problem. There was another, more serious. On take-off, as the aircraft forged ahead under full power across the airfield, the propeller whipped up mud, sending it flying into the air intake, clogging the radiator and spattering the underside of the wings and fuselage. Mud was the most likely culprit when Paul Arbon's Hurricane crashed on take-off. Paul, a pale-faced and slightly plump young man, was nicknamed 'Dopey' -- why I never understood, because there was nothing about his flying that suggested he was particularly dim-witted. On the contrary, he was an able pilot and loyal friend. When his engine cut just as he was lifting his Hurricane off the ground it careered into a Nissen hut occupied by ground-crew. Dopey emerged from the wreckage unhurt, but five men inside the hut were injured when the three tons of Hurricane descended upon them.

Gravesend, true to its name, witnessed the very nadir of our fortunes. We soon found out that our new VHF radio sets were not reliable. If the causes were obscure, the effect played on the morale of our pilots. Map-reading in the total dark of the black-out being out of the question, the night-fighter pilot depended on the ground controller to guide him home. Homing by radio was his assurance of a safe return to base; if he was deprived of it for some reason he was hopelessly lost -- unless he was lucky, as I was the night that my radio packed up somewhere over Kent. The slender crescent of the moon gave but a dim light, but visibility was good. I soon picked out the coastline, then laboriously followed it up the Thames estuary until I spotted the red flashing beacon of Gravesend. These light-houses were sited some five miles from the airfield and flashed in Morse the two 'letters of the night'. Site and letters were changed nightly. They were a godsend to us, but the Germans were for a long time puzzled by them, occasionally bombing them out of sheer frustration. Had the weather been thick that night my last hope would have been to bale out — still a chancy business, for it was impossible to know where you would fall, on terra firma or in the drink, where in the icy water you were likely to perish. Many unfortunate Luftwaffe crews, equipped though they were with dinghies, radio and survival rations and pills, suffered such a fate. Their bodies were washed up in numbers on the east and south coast. For both sides weather and sea were common foes.

On the night of 8 December the Luftwaffe, more than 400 bombers strong, returned to the assault on London. They blasted the city with hundreds of tons of high explosive and more than a hundred thousand incendiary bombs, raising fires which inflamed the sky above and shed enough light on Gravesend to read a newspaper. Many of us, myself included, were dispatched during that awful night to do battle with the hidden enemy, but in vain. The controller positioned me to patrol at 16,000 feet between the estuary and the city itself. It was tormenting, in all that immensity of black sky, to look down on London three miles beneath me, consumed by fire and torn by the blast of bombs and landmines whose fiery conflagrations rent the darkness below. For two hours, while the enemy was killing hundreds of our people, I searched in vain, desperate and ashamed at our impotence to defend the defenceless.

Having landed, taxied in and switched off, I jumped down from the cockpit sick at heart, and walked through the mud to the floodlight. That night the wind was westerly and the flare-path was laid out so that we landed towards London. Sergeant Calderwood was approaching to land. A ruddy-faced young

Irishman with a pleasing brogue, he was a steady pilot and as we were about to see, a man of selfless courage. His approach seemed normal, but as he flashed past the floodlight I could see that he was going too fast. His wheels touched well down the flare-path; he squeezed the brake lever on the control column, slid, wheels locked, across the mud and tore into the tangle of barbed wire forming the airfield defences. The Hurricane's tail reared into the air as it overturned and came finally to rest on its back.

With others I ran to the scene, but in our frantic efforts to reach the Hurricane and its pilot the clawing barbed wire ripped our clothing and held us back. A strong smell of petrol was in the air, and I well knew that a crashed Hurricane could lie inert for a minute or two, then burst into flames. The suspense was agonizing. I was hung up in the barbed wire and quite close to Calderwood, but incapable of getting closer. I told him 'Hold on, the firemen will soon cut you out.' Never did his Irish brogue affect me more than when he answered calmly, 'Don't worry about me, take care o' yourselves.' He might have been incinerated within the next few minutes, but thankfully the Hurricane did not go up in flames. The firemen extricated our Irishman, redder in the face than usual after hanging on his straps for twenty minutes upside down.

Two nights of foul weather brought a short respite to London and the provinces. We nevertheless continued to patrol. With the low-lying clouds, full of lightning and reflecting the searchlight beams below, flying was extremely unpleasant, not to say risky. Around midnight Sergeant Hutton, a quiet, stolid young Yorkshireman, took his turn to patrol. He had not been gone more than half an hour when I was informed that an aircraft, probably a Hurricane, had crashed in Tilbury docks, just opposite us on the north bank of the river. After a roundabout journey by car through Deptford Tunnel I at last found the place, a deep, gaping hole in the soft ground wherein were embedded all but a few remnants of a Hurricane. Men had been working with flares and a lifting rig to haul out the wreckage — and with it the body of poor Hutton. After some hours the foreman said to me: 'It's no good, we'll never reach him. All we can do is to fill in the hole.' 'Keep on trying,' I pleaded. 'He deserves a decent burial.' This Hutton finally received when, ten days later, his body was recovered.

Some people say 'Never two without three.' Such was to be 85 Squadron's misfortune during those ghastly nights at Gravesend. Sergeant Howes, a calm, loyal member of our band, had fought with them in France and been shot down. Now he was back with us, but stayed barely long enough to meet up again with his old friends. One freezing night just before Christmas, when clouds hung low, he apparently lost control of his aircraft and dived into the ground. The cause of the tragedy may well have been icing; or it may have been that he was confused by lightning and searchlights. We were never to know, for our good friend died without a word on the radio. They had carried his body away before I reached the burnt-out wreckage of his Hurricane, beside which lay a charred, pathetic-looking flying-boot.

Gravesend was giving us a cruel time, but there was no dismay, not even among the youngest like Sergeant Gray, who looked more like a boy of sixteen than a skilful and determined night-fighter pilot. His daring exploits in bad weather sometimes alarmed me, and I would wait anxiously on the flare-path for his return. Another youthful but more seasoned pilot was Jim Bailey, who had fought by day in Defiants and was lucky to be alive. You would never have imagined that he was the son of a millionaire father, Sir Abe, for Jim usually had at least one hole in his trousers and drove around in a rickety little Morris 8. His fair hair was perpetually dishevelled and he was always laughing — at what or at whom I was not always sure, but I often suspected it was me. He had flying in his blood; his mother was a well-known and intrepid aviatrice.

With Jim Bailey came his friend Bill Carnaby, another survivor of the carnage of the Defiants. Tall, dark, thin and taciturn, Bill was the very opposite to his friend Jim, but a most welcome addition to our ranks, whose remaining gaps were being filled by seasoned volunteer pilots. Another was Dudley Honor, who had fought valiantly in Greece. Shot down behind the enemy lines, he made good his escape and was taken off from an isolated beach by an RAF flying-boat.

Gus Gowers was another old hand who returned to 85 Squadron. He had fought in France and in the Battle of Britain, when he was shot down. Burnt on the face and hands, he was taken to Caterham Mental Hospital, a wing of which had been given over to the RAF. It was there, on my own release from hospital, that I had visited Gus. His face was still black, and his burnt fingers like claws. Yet for all that he could not get over the joke of ending up in a 'loony bin'. Neither, as soon became sadly apparent, had he yet got over the shock of his terrible wounds. Soon after he came back to us he confessed as much to me; he could not take it — yet. He left us for a temporary ground job and I never saw him again. Later, while leading a day-fighter squadron over France, Gus was killed.

The same fate overcame our French friends, Émile and François. The language problem having proved too difficult, they left us for day-fighters. Before leaving, Émile wrote to me. *'Nous étions parmi vous absolument comme chez nous. L'Escadrille était notre "Home" . . . maintenant, plus que jamais nous sommes certains d'avoir la victoire'* (Among you we were absolutely as if among our own. The Squadron was our 'Home' . . . now we are more than ever certain of victory.) Émile was killed leading a RAF squadron over Dieppe in 1942. François disappeared during an offensive patrol over his own country.

One evening after putting my Hurricane through the usual night test, I returned to Jeskyn's for a bite before the hour of 'readiness'. There, sitting in a chair in the drawing-room, I found an elderly-looking gentleman, his wavy grey hair parted down the middle, his narrow rubicund face aglow with good health. My attention was immediately drawn to his pilot's wings and the medal ribbons below them — the Military Cross and two campaign medals of the First World War. 'Good evening, sir,' I said politely. 'Good evening, sir,' he replied, with an embarrassed smile. It was only then that I noticed the thin stripe of a pilot officer on his sleeves. He went on, 'You must be the CO of 85

Squadron. I'm reporting to you for flying duties. My name is Wheeler.'

James Wheeler was a prodigious personage. As a young soldier in the first war, the two smaller fingers of his left hand had been shot away. He managed to hold the throttle lever perfectly well with his remaining two fingers and thumb, and like this had done thousands of hours' flying as an airline pilot. Although I never discovered his exact age, it was somewhere well into the forties. We continued to call each other 'sir' for a while. Then I came to call him James and he, to my relief, dropped the 'sir'.

Our losses and our pains and frustrations never dampened the spirits of the wonderful team of which I happened to be the leader. We would have to keep on groping in the dark with our dear Hurricanes until equipped with proper, 'specialized' night-fighters. The only type at present in existence was the Beaufighter, priority for which was naturally given to the six Blenheim night-fighter squadrons. The Beaufighter, its teething troubles remedied, promised to be a scourge of the enemy's bombers. The night after Sergeant Howe died, John Cunningham and Sergeant Phillipson scored another decisive victory, this time against a Heinkel 111 of Kampfgruppe 100.

19

FOUL WEATHER

December was what Londoners, with tactful understatement, were calling a 'light month', although it was to end with a holocaust. They all — the Callow family included — were able to enjoy a short breather while the Luftwaffe was concentrating its night offensive against our ports and industrial cities.

Sheffield was one of them. The city came under heavy attack on the 12th of December and again on the 15th. It was bad luck on Melve Callow, the wag of the family, that she arrived that very day in Sheffield with friends to attend the twenty-first birthday party of a football star, Bill Pickering. She had hesitated before going but her mother encouraged her: 'Go on, Melve, it will make a nice change for you.' So Melve dressed up in her beautiful pale blue costume, which she had recently bought and was saving for the party.

When her train pulled into Sheffield station Melve saw that it was in ruins — hit during the raid three nights earlier. She and her friends made straight for Bill Pickering's house, where guests were already arriving. As a precaution, each one was first shown down to the basement shelter. Then up to the ground floor again where the party started. Just as it was in full swing the sirens began wailing, and all but a few of the guests trooped down to the shelter. Melve was among those who stayed outside to keep company with one of her London friends, Harry, who had been injured in the London bombing and was on crutches.

At the height of the raid a bomb demolished the house next door, sending an avalanche of debris down the shelter stairs and blocking the entrance. Ironically, those few who had stayed outside were unhurt; they all, except for lame, unfortunate Harry, began digging with their bare hands to free the trapped revellers who, as they staggered out bleeding and dishevelled, threw their arms for support round the first person they met. By the time they were all out Melve's beautiful pale blue costume was torn and stained with blood and dust. Ambulances took the shelter victims away, leaving Harry with his crutches and Melve in her rags, sitting disconsolately among the rubble. 'Blimey', complained Melve, 'they might bleedin' well have taken us with them.' Next day, still in her rags, she hastened back to London.

A few nights before Christmas the Luftwaffe turned once again on Liverpool and its docks on the river Mersey which, with Glasgow's Clydeside docks, were the terminus of Britain's lifeline with America and Canada. They were back the following night in greater strength — 300 bombers with the usual mixture of high explosive and incendiaries. The series continued during two more nights, when it was the turn of Manchester to be ravaged by blast and fire. Next day was the eve of Christmas with its message of goodwill among men, which men, whether at war or not, had always so barely heeded. During the festival itself, however, the bombardment was interrupted — more probably because of the forbidding weather, which kept us pinned to the ground, than for any feelings of good will that Hitler and his bloody henchmen may have felt for the British.

Christmas and Boxing Day over, the Luftwaffe on Friday 27 December came to London bringing their gifts of oil-bombs, explosive and fire. The night was well chosen, for city workers had gone for the week-end leaving offices, shops and warehouses unwatched. At Gravesend a dense haze reduced horizontal visibility to zero and clamped us to the ground. Once again powerless to intervene, we could only watch the white vapour trails streaming behind the bombers heading up the estuary for

London, hear the sickening thud of their bombs and gaze sadly at the fiery glow lighting up London's sky.

That raid was a prelude to the great city fire of Sunday the 29th — a night yet more favourable to the fire-raisers when the Thames, the source of the firemen's water-supply, was at its lowest — a thin river bounded on each side by a broad stretch of stinking slush, through which the firemen had to haul their connecting hoses in order to draw on the saving water.

That raid was made by less than 150 bombers, and by 10 p.m. was called off because of bad weather over the Luftwaffe's bases. But Kampfgruppe 100 who led it, navigating on X-Gerät, their Heinkels loaded with incendiaries only, accomplished their mission as 'path-finders' with precise and deadly effect. Although they were already alive to the disturbing influences of 'Bromide', the RAF's jammer, it failed to upset their aim that night. They laid down a carpet of fire within a radius of about one mile from St Paul's. Visible from afar, despite the broken cloud drifting over London, it beckoned as at Coventry to the rest of the pack, who had only to stoke the flames with their high-explosive and incendiary bombs. The burning city kindled into a huge brazier. Nothing like it had been seen since the Great Fire of 1666, when the diarist John Evelyn wrote that he witnessed 'a blood red sky, painted by a myriad of seething fires'.

Nearly three centuries later young Ray Callow, doing his duty as a messenger that night, had a similar vision. 'It looked as if the whole City was on fire and the sky above as well.' It did not seem to him that London could be saved. But the firemen were as ever fighting back against the devouring flames. Ray's brother Johnny was there. It was not until towards the end of that brief, devastating raid that the bells went down at the Earldom Square substation. 'Numbers one and two pumps!' The keen rivalry between Johnny's No. 1 pump and his friend Steve Needham's No. 2 put them on their mettle as they raced each other up the Old Kent Road, heading for Blackfriars Bridge. At one moment Pat Mahoney, No. 3 in Johnny's team, cried out: 'Heh, look, up there!' Above, they could clearly see aircraft silhouetted against the incandescent sky. Then they were crossing Blackfriars

Bridge and, turning right, came to Ludgate Hill, to be faced with the inspiring, unforgettable spectacle of St Paul's cathedral, its famous dome with the Cross high aloft, standing proud of the surrounding smoke and flames — London's cathedral, the symbol of London's indomitable resistance.

The main load of bombs dropped within that circle around St Paul's marked by KGr 100's incendiaries. A strong westerly wind fanned the flames, until between the cathedral and the Guildhall there raged an impassable sea of fire. More conflagrations were devouring the area bounded by Moorgate, Aldersgate, Old Street and Cannon Street. Many of London's ancient and cherished architectural treasures were vandalized that night. Bombs struck the County Hall and the Tower of London, and the Guildhall, heart of London's pride and tradition, was half consumed by fire. Eight Wren churches were shattered and burnt. But in the midst of all that desolation Wren's great masterpiece, St Paul's, stood up defiant and practically unscathed.

The evening out of Johnny and his team ended in anticlimax. Although hundreds of pumps had converged on the city, some fires were so fierce that they had to be left to burn themselves out. Ordered to stand by, Johnny's team did so until dawn, when the fire-control officer told them 'You can push off.' Neither wet nor dirty, they drove back dejected to the substation, there to be greeted with jibes: 'Well, mates, where've you all been? Out on a beano or something?'

Dejected too were the pilots of 85 Squadron who had flown off into the night in an attempt to engage the enemy with the aid of the system called 'Layers'. While the AA guns held their fire, 'cats-eye' fighters were 'stacked up' at intervals of 500 feet to patrol above the blazing city in the hope of spotting an enemy bomber against the flames. But the bombers seen that night from the ground by Pat Mahoney and his comrades of No. 1 Pump remained, in the confusion of smoke and cloud, invisible to our pilots above.

Thus 85 Squadron made its last vain effort in 1940 to defend London by night. Our failure did not come from want of trying; we had put in more hours of flying than any other squadron. It was due to lack of the right tools. In an attempt to bolster up the ineffective night defences, weird devices — brain-children of the boffins — had recently been tried. One was the aerial mine. Carried by old-fashioned Handley Page Harrow aircraft to 20,000 feet — it took them an hour to get there — the mines, which dangled from a parachute on the end of 2000 feet of wire, were sown across the path of approaching enemy bombers. An ingenious but fruitless idea. A more crazy one was proposed by the Navy, experts at sowing mines at sea but less realistic about their possibilities for ensnaring enemy bombers. The sailors' plan was to release scores of free balloons, each with an explosive charge attached, to drift with the wind toward the advancing bombers. But the wind bloweth where it listeth: the drifting explosives might end up anywhere. The idea was soon abandoned, fortunately for the continued well-being of our own flyers.

Yet another idea, one for use on the ground, was the decoy fire devised by Colonel John Turner, onetime director of Air Ministry Works and Buildings and affectionately known, if I am not mistaken, as 'Concrete Bill'. The purpose of his decoy fires (called 'Starfish' sites) was to draw the main bomber force away from the fires raised by the pathfinders of KGr 100. Starfish sites had harvested a good number of bombs, and were to gather many more.

With all these thoughts and visions of impeding the enemy came the news that we were to be re-equipped with Defiants, the two-seater ex-day fighter with a four-gun turret. Although the news stirred no particular enthusiasm among us, we felt willing to try any machine which might be an improvement, as a night-fighter, on our well-loved Hurricane day-fighters. The Defiant was clearly not the ultimate solution but a stepping-stone perhaps to something better. Despite my deep and lingering instincts of a day-fighter pilot, flying a single-seater, single-engine plane, I felt certain that only a machine fitted with radar, with an operator to work it — that meant a two-seater, twin-engined aircraft — could provide the answer to interception at night. The proof had been amply demonstrated by John Cunningham and

John Phillipson in their Beaufighter. Before reaching that ideal we would have to grope blindly in the dark, cold winter skies for many a night, disappointed by our continuing failure but by no means demoralized.

As the year drew to a close, with London still smouldering, the British prime minister Winston Churchill was far from being dejected. He felt on the contrary that 'all this clatter and storm' was a stimulant to further effort. Looking back on 1940, he saw it as a 'tremendous year', if the most deadly in British history. The 'citadel of the Commonwealth' had defied the enemy's attempts to take it by storm.

Beyond the seas, it is true, British positions were dangerously menaced, and her Army, Air Force and above all her Navy and Merchant Navy were stretched to the limit. But they still held on, and when occasion arose — as it did more and more — fought back. Malta, hitherto defenceless but a potential thorn in Italy's side, was reinforced by convoys sailing in the face of the Italian navy and air force.

The Italian invasion of Greece (to whom Britain had pledged her aid, however slender it might be) had been repulsed by the Greek army. Suda Bay, the best harbour in Crete, was occupied, with the Greeks' assent, by the British navy, who sailed on a few days later to cripple the Italian fleet at Taranto.

On the far shore of the Mediterranean, in North Africa, the 25,000 strong British Army of the Nile had repulsed the Italian advance into Egypt, taking 38,000 prisoners. With their meagre, dispersed forces the British were so far holding their own in the eastern Mediterranean, while their naval Force H took care of the western end.

Only one thing, Churchill said, ever frightened him: the German U-boat menace, and that was not quite all. At the end of October the German pocket-battleship *Admiral Scheer* broke out, via the Denmark Strait north of Iceland, into the Atlantic. A month later she was followed by the heavy cruiser *Admiral Hipper*. Both warships began to prey on British convoys. During a five months' cruise *Scheer* sank sixteen merchantmen. *Hipper*, intercepted by the Royal Navy early in her career, had to run for

Brest. But the battle-cruisers *Scharnhorst* and *Gneisenau*, and the pocket-battleships *Tirpitz* and *Bismarck*, were lurking in port, waiting to join the marauders.

The U-boats presented a more deadly peril. Invisible (when they chose to be), evasive and in great numbers, they had the immense strategic advantage of ports on the north and west coast of France. The British, on the other hand, denied ports and airfields in the neutral Irish Republic, had to divert their convoys around Northern Ireland through the North-Western Approaches, to Liverpool's Merseyside and Glasgow's Clydeside. These two ports, as Churchill said, were now of mortal significance.

During one week in September U-boats sank twenty-seven ships. In October twenty out of a convoy of thirty-four were sent to the bottom by U-boats. Imports of oil, food and equipment declined, but still the massacre of the brave merchant ships went on until one night in December, when the U-boat scourge was at its most cruel, Churchill called a meeting in the downstairs War-Room in Whitehall. Only senior naval officers were present. Out of the tense discussion came the decision to go over to the offensive. From now on RAF Coastal Command and naval anti-submarine craft would relentlessly hunt the U-boats in the very waters they had chosen to hunt out convoys. The Battle of the Atlantic entered a new phase.

Churchill, himself half American through his mother, kept in constant touch with the American president Franklin D. Roosevelt, signing himself nostalgically as 'Former Naval Person'. Ceaselessly he apprised the president of Britain's grievous losses in ships bringing arms, equipment and food to the beleaguered island. The mortal danger to Britain, he wrote, was the diminution in shipping tonnage. 'We can endure the shattering of our dwellings and the slaughter of our civil population', he wrote, but unless there were ships enough 'to feed the island, import munitions and move armies . . . we may fall by the way'.

Churchill had to face the stark fact that Britain, up to November 1940, had paid $4,500,000,000 in cash for American aid, and was nearing the bottom of the barrel. Only $200,000,000 was left. He told the president frankly: 'The more rapid and abundant the flow of munitions and ships which you are able to send us, the sooner our dollar supply will be exhausted.' This did not deter him from placing an immediate order for 2000 combat planes a month, confident as he said that the Americans would not limit their generous aid only to what Britain could pay for. 'You may be certain', he promised, 'that we shall prove ourselves ready to suffer and sacrifice to the utmost for the Cause and that we glory in being its champions.'

Months earlier Mrs Eleanor Roosevelt had remarked, with exceeding candour, to her husband: 'You must remember, Britain represents our first line of defence.' Now the president, on 17 December was almost repeating her words, as he told a press conference: 'There is absolutely no doubt in the mind of a very overwhelming number of Americans that the best immediate defence of the United States is the success of Great Britain defending itself.' Both for that reason and for the survival of democracy, he concluded, America should do everything possible to help the British.

Thus was born (or rather reborn) the idea of Lend-Lease, for the concept originated in a US government statute dating back to 1892, permitting the Secretary of War to lease army property 'when, in his discretion, it will be for the public good'. The new Lend-Lease Bill was prepared for Congress — Churchill described it as 'the most unsordid act in the history of any nation'. President Roosevelt — 'our great friend', as Churchill called him — in his 'fireside chat' on 30 December, told the American nation: 'There is danger ahead . . . If Britain should go down all of us in the Americas would be living at the point of a gun . . . We must produce arms and ships. . . . We must be the great arsenal of Democracy.'

Thus Britain was now free to plan, unshackled by debt and doubt for the future. Churchill explained, 'What we had was lent or leased to us because our continued resistance to the Hitler tyranny was deemed to be of vital interest to the great Republic.'

It is always remarkable how one particular topic can be the

subject of so many divergent opinions — especially when the political gentry are involved. By the end of 1940 Churchill was certain of ultimate victory, however bitter the struggle. His gallant if exacting ally General de Gaulle confided to his close collaborators *'La guerre est gagnée'* — the war is won. Almost the same words were used by the German foreign minister, Ribbentrop, in a letter to Germany's ally, the Russian dictator Stalin: 'The war has been won by us,' he wrote. 'It is only a question of how long it will be before England . . . admits to collapse.' And Stalin expressed his readiness to share in the resultant spoils of this now overdue event. Shortly afterwards Hitler, unrivalled as a political double-crosser, issued in mid-December his Directive No. 12, headed 'Operation Barbarossa', whose purpose was 'to crush Soviet Russia in a quick campaign before the end of the war against England'. The Fuehrer on New Year's Eve wrote to his friend, the Italian dictator Benito Mussolini, assuring him 'The war in the west is itself won. A violent effort is still necessary to crush England.'

But it was Molotov, the poker-faced Russian commissar for foreign affairs, who together with Churchill undoubtedly had the best grip on the situation. After days of stormy meetings with Ribbentrop and Hitler in Berlin, he gave a farewell banquet. Just as Ribbentrop rose to answer a toast of friendship the sirens started wailing and the guests hurried down to the basement shelter, where the two foreign ministers continued their talks. Churchill later wrote: 'We had heard of the conference beforehand and though not invited to join in the discussion did not wish to be entirely left out of the proceedings.' Indeed, RAF bombers were at the rendezvous. While they cruised overhead, the explosions of their bombs reverberating to the depths of the shelter, Ribbentrop kept repeating to Molotov that Britain was finished. 'If that is so,' replied the commissar, 'why are we in this shelter and whose are those bombs which fall?'

20

ICING UP

Early in the new year 85 Squadron migrated to Debden, our familiar habitat north of London where we enjoyed the luxury of metalled runways. There, thanks to the dense fog which kept us grounded, we were able to preen our ruffled feathers. During this month and the next, fog, ice, snow and low-lying cloud was to prevent both the enemy and ourselves from flying — the kind of weather when one said 'Even the birds have to walk.'

Bad weather was an obstacle, a physical one, to which we were now well accustomed. The arrival in our midst of Defiants, with air-gunners to fit, was more a psychological problem. The Defiant was powered with the same Rolls-Royce Merlin engine as were our Hurricanes. It was a sound aircraft, but it was considerably slower than the Hurricane and also, of course, a two-seater. We had fought successfully by day and fumbled by night as single-seater pilots in a high-performance machine. Now we were obliged to fly an inferior machine, not as captains of our own little ship, but as taxi-drivers to the air gunner behind, ensconced in his four-gun turret. We all tried to believe that this combination would improve our results as night-fighters, the ultimate aim. Despite my own unspoken doubts and theirs we were agreed that we would go ahead and try. If in Defiants we could do better at night than in Hurricanes, that would be our reward. 'The prospect of losing the Hurricanes', our adjutant wrote in the squadron diary, 'was directly responsible for many impromptu aerobatic displays.' But our Hurricanes were not immediately taken from us. While we practised by day and by night in Defiants, we flew Hurricanes on operational night patrols — as usual in vain, even on the nights of the 11th and 12th, when London came under heavy attack. On the tarmac that night I was chatting with Sergeant Calderwell. Pointing southward towards a red glow in the sky, he remarked, 'Look at the moon rising; what a marvellous sight!' 'That's not the moon,' I told him. 'It's London burning.'

In mid-January our commander-in-chief, Air Marshal Sholto Douglas, paid us a visit. Of medium stature, eagle-eyed, eagle-nosed and extremely sharp-witted, he was a chief to whom you could speak your mind with the certainty of being listened to attentively. We gathered about him in the pilots' room and he talked to us in turn. When I presented James Wheeler, Sholto paused a moment in front of this grey-haired veteran with first world war medals. 'How old are you, Wheeler?' he asked. 'Thirty-five, sir,' replied James, unabashed. 'Really?' pursued Sholto. 'You must have been a pretty remarkable child in the first world war.'

James was still a remarkable man. With his age and experience, I always knew I could count on his help when needed. That night, with the cloud base at 300 feet, the enemy were droning thousands of feet overhead on their way to bomb the Rolls-Royce works at Derby. Although he had grounded us because of the weather, the controller telephoned, asking tentatively for a 'weather test'. My maxim being 'Never ask others to do anything you can't do yourself', I took the hairiest weather tests upon myself. Tearing down the runway in my Hurricane and up into the dark, I was immediately enveloped in cloud. Climbing still, I soon broke out into a crystal-clear sky studded with stars. So beautiful was it that I would gladly have stayed there all night, but as the low cloud made operations impossible, my immediate problem was to get down safely to the airfield. Rather than take the risk of blinding down through the cloud and ending up in a heap on the ground, I spoke to the controller: 'Wagon Leader calling, please ask Pilot Officer Wheeler in officers' mess to go quickly to control tower and call me.'

James, off duty and peacefully sipping a beer, responded immediately. Five minutes later he called me. 'Hullo, Wagon Leader . . .' 'Hullo, James', I replied, 'please fire off a few rockets [they rose to 1,000 feet] to help me position airfield. Tell local searchlights to project horizontally so that I can see the ground.' One after another rockets came shooting up through the cloud layer and faded out. At the fourth volley I was close enough to the airfield to begin my descent. Confident in our joint technique, I let down into the cloud. Seconds passed, and then suddenly I was in the full glare of the horizontal beams, and trees and telegraph posts were flashing past just below. And there was Debden's flashing beacon. The rest was easy; our makeshift method had worked perfectly. It only remained for me to offer James a final beer.

The main satisfaction we got from our Defiants was giving our faithful and efficient ground-crews an occasional joy-ride. They were always close to us pilots, and shared in our tribulations. But we made slow progress in becoming operational on the new aircraft. Snow and fog kept us grounded for nights on end. There was another reason, too: a rumour had reached me that we were soon to be re-equipped with Havocs, the British name given to the American twin-engined Douglas DB7, originally a high-performance medium bomber but now being converted in Britain into a night-fighter with AI and a battery of eight machine-guns in the nose. Confirmation soon came from Air Vice Marshal Leigh-Mallory, now commanding No. 11 Group, who had been following our problems closely and heeding my repeated pleas for better equipment. It looked as if we were on the verge of becoming specialized night-fighters.

For us the era of the Defiant was over. It was not to be despised as a cats-eye night-fighter, and as such the Luftwaffe found it a troublesome and determined adversary, especially in attacks from below, when the plan view of the bomber offered a larger target to the Defiant's air-gunner. This solid but shapely machine made a useful contribution to the gradually increasing respect generated among the Luftwaffe for British night-fighters. If the Defiant did not find favour with us, it did help to convert us from the single-seater mentality to the two-seater. There remained yet another step, from single-engined aircraft to twin-engined, with AI — the answer to the night-fighter's prayer.

In mid-January John Cunningham (with Sergeant Jimmy Rawnsley, now his radar operator) downed another enemy bomber. Their interception was an all-time classic; perfect co-operation of the GCI whose controller, Flight Lieutenant Brown, put John within AI range of the enemy, and AI which enabled Rawnsley to guide his pilot to within visual distance. GCI stations were going up all over the country. Our own, in the Debden sector, was at Waldringfield, in Suffolk. We had already started working with it, but in Hurricanes we still lacked the missing link, AI, which once ours would connect us directly with the enemy. As we waited for Havocs we continued our lone patrols in Hurricanes, for as long as snow and fog did not keep us and the Luftwaffe earth-bound.

Just before the month ended their Majesties the King and Queen paid us the honour of a visit. The King and Queen moved tirelessly among their bombed-out subjects and fighting-men, who took courage from their Majesties' obviously genuine concern for their well-being. Douglas Bader's 242 Canadian squadron had come over from near-by Duxford for the occasion. Douglas, five years my senior in age, was a human phenomenon. With one leg amputated above the knee, the other just below, he was yet one of the greatest of our fighter pilots. The officers and men of our two squadrons were ranged stiffly inside a hangar. Just before the arrival of their Majesties, Douglas (whom I had first known during the day-fighting) confided to me, 'Look, old boy [his standard opening gambit], the one thing I can't do is stand properly to attention. So if I overbalance, please come to the rescue.' As the royal inspection proceeded I waited nervously for Douglas, tin legs and all, to crash to the ground. Luckily, by parting his feet slightly, he remained upright.

It was a long tradition, originating probably from the RAF's origins in 1918, for 'fighter boys' to wear the top button of their blue uniform tunic undone. When one or two pilots had asked me 'Should we do it up for the King?' I replied, 'No, let's keep up the old tradition.' So all our pilots' top buttons remained undone. Douglas evidently had a more proper respect for royal protocol; all his pilots' top buttons were done up. The King — who had a keen eye for details of dress — came to our pilots, stopped in front of Sammy Allard and asked him: 'Why do the pilots in your squadron wear their top buttons undone and the other squadron's are done up?' Sammy, with his disarming grin, replied 'It's an old tradition, sir. Perhaps the others are too shy of your Majesty.' Standing behind the King, our dear commander-in-chief, Sholto Douglas, went very red in the face.

'Come February, fill dyke, be it black or be it white.' True to the old adage, February gave us a generous downpour of both, keeping Luftwaffe night-bombers and RAF night-fighters out of the sky. Only two major raids were made that month, both on the Welsh port of Swansea.

Our most insidious enemy was as usual the weather. Geoff Howitt, caught in a snow-storm, managed to grope his way into Gravesend, of all places. Sergeant Webster, an exceptionally able young pilot, ran into double trouble — a snowstorm and engine-failure. By a miracle he survived a crash-landing.

Suddenly one night the sky cleared and sparkled with stars. Back came the Luftwaffe, though not in force. 'Dopey' Arbon was first off on patrol. The GCI controller put him on to an enemy bomber, guiding him so accurately that in the clear sky he came close enough to sight it. He opened fire, only to see the enemy aircraft dive away and disappear. I was next off. Hardly having lifted away from the airfield, I was fired upon by some unseen enemy lurking in the dark. I called for a 'vector', and the sector controller gave me a course to steer which, lacking the accuracy of the GCI, failed to put me on the track of the intruder. Such incidents only increased our frustration and made us long all the more for Havocs. They also warned us that German night-fighters on offensive patrol were prowling in the dark around us. We had not forgotten that semi-comic adventure at Kirton four months ago. The German offensive patrols were operating out of Schiphol, in Holland, and although mainly on the look-out for returning RAF bombers, would not hesitate to attack anything in the air or on the ground. Ju 88s and Dornier 17s had been converted into night-fighters, each with a forward-firing 20 mm cannon and machine-guns.

In Germany night-fighter pilots had not yet caught the public imagination. Their defensive cats-eye night-fighters, in Me 109s and Me 110s, operated like us by single patrols, limited only to thirty minutes to an hour, with no more than three per night. We were worked harder, naturally, since our country was under heavier attack. Controlled by R/T, and with searchlights indicating the raiders, the German pilots — again like us — realized that it needed a lot of luck to bring off an interception. The general opinion was that night-flying was at best a thankless job, at worst a nightmare, and costly in pilots' lives. Stronger opinions were held by Italian pilots: night-fighters were useless, AA guns being more effective. A pilot of the Regia Aeronautica who had gone up in pitch-dark against an RAF attack on Turin thought he was lucky to get down alive. However much we could sympathize with all these feelings, it was meanwhile clear that besides pursuing our bombers, German night-fighters on offensive patrol were also interested in us. If the compliment was hardly deserved, it was all the same rather flattering.

There came to us at this time to gain experience a wing-commander from the Air Ministry named Hamilton, tall, charming and, after years spent behind an office desk, slightly haggard. To have quit its safety for the glorious uncertainties of night-fighting proved that he was a brave man. I was watching on the tarmac one night as, navigation lights on (as was the rule), Hamilton approached to land. Suddenly out of the darkness came a long burst of machine-gun fire, followed by the roar of a zooming aircraft — another of those German night-fighters. He missed our friend, who wisely extinguished his lights and after waiting a while landed intact.

The cold of these winter nights put us to almost unendurable torture, our black, long-suffering Hurricanes as well. At high altitude the temperature inside the cockpit was no more than a few degrees above the arctic temperatures outside. Various means were proposed by our thoughtful scientists to alleviate our discomfort: for our flying-boots inner soles, filled with a chemical which when water was added through a little hole gave off heat. A nice idea, but the thick inner sole made the boots a tight and uncomfortable fit. More popular were 'hot potatoes', bags filled with the same chemical which you slipped into any available pocket. They too were somewhat cumbersome. We tried an electrically heated flying-suit, only to discard it, for it was too bulky for the small confines of the cockpit. German Me109 pilots did likewise with theirs. The Sidcot flying-suit (a relic of the first war) helped to keep out the cold for those who liked to wear it, but in the cockpit it was hampering. I preferred to pile on as many sweaters as there was room for. Silk and wool were the best thermal insulators. Generous Americans, moved by our country's resistance, sent over 'Bundles for Britain', no doubt in the same Atlantic convoys as were bringing our Havocs. Among them, apart from Balaclava helmets, scarves and other woollies to wear on the ground, was a kind of home-knitted sleeve which could stretch from the leg over the knee and up to the thigh. It took up no room, and greatly helped to save our lower limbs from frostbite. In one of my own limbs the left leg and foot — which in the day-fighting had 'stopped' a hefty German bullet — the blood circulation was not so good, and the cold numbed it up to the knee. A pair of silk stockings sent by my mother went a long way to alleviate the problem. To protect their hands some pilots wore leather gauntlets, but I preferred to feel with my fingers the touch of the controls and switches. Woollen mittens over thin silk gloves kept my hands warm enough.

In the intense cold at high altitude our Hurricanes suffered too. You could feel the throttle lever and controls stiffening in the freezing air. Ice forming on the air intake and propeller blades made the engine falter and sent vibrations through the aircraft and into your body, which was part of it. Ice building up on the leading edges of wings and tail-plane altered their profile and impaired their 'lift', leaving you with a horrible sinking feeling which you could not control unless you dived down to a lower altitude. But this manœuvre, while a remedy to one problem, provoked another. The humidity in the air lower down formed an opaque layer of ice on the thick frozen glass of the bullet-proof windscreen. Coming in to land one night in February with my windscreen completely obscured, I had to open the hood, and sliding my left hand forward along the side panel of the windscreen, to scrape the ice off the front of it with my nails in order to see the flare-path.

We possessed but one remedy to prevent icing: a thick, sticky brown paste which was rubbed on the propeller, air intake and the leading edges of the wings. It was the invention, so they said, of an imaginative but not too realistic boffin, who remarking that snowdrops did not freeze up, concocted this paste from their flowers. It sounded like a tall story.

Naturally, the Germans also endured similar problems from the bitter cold. For clearing snow from the runway they found the tri-motor Junkers 52 (if there was one available) effective as it taxied up and down, blowing away the snow in the slipstream of its three propellers. A more serious problem was the icing up in flight of their planes. Several had crashed, some of them in Britain. German de-icing equipment was not standard, some aircraft being fitted with pulsating systems to prevent formation of ice, others with a system that blew hot air through pipes in the leading edge of wings. These somewhat sophisticated systems were supplemented by a special de-icing paste that was hardly likely (given the Germans' know-how in synthetic chemistry) to have been made from snowdrops. It was rubbed on by hand by the ground staff, but some aircrew, not trusting their technical men, did the dirty work themselves.

While both air forces quailed before the rigours of winter, as the Luftwaffe pursued their mission of destruction against our cities and ports they had to face perils as bad, if not worse, as those of the elements. As already described, the RAF's radio counter-offensive had sown much confusion among the enemy. The jammer 'Aspirin' had thoroughly calmed the Luftwaffe's enthusiasm for Knickebein: aircrews could not trust that particular beam navigation system any longer. The precision of X-Gerät, the beam used by the fire-lighters Kampfgruppe 100, had been so blurred by our 'Bromide' jammers that those celebrated Luftwaffe pathfinders were evidently no longer happy in their work — fiddling with their frequencies in the middle of an attack in an effort to escape from 'Bromide', and on one occasion dropping parachute-mines which could not possibly be aimed to mark the target with any accuracy.

The Luftwaffe's latest and most sophisticated in beam systems, Y-Gerät, fitted in the Heinkels of Kampfgeschwader 26's 3rd Staffel, proved a fiasco from the start. Since its signals had first been detected in November 1940 by the RAF's Y-service, Dr Cockburn had been working on his jammer, 'Domino'. The BBC, with their powerful television transmitter at Alexandra Palace in south London, were also in the plot, re-radiating the German signal and causing turmoil with their ingenious but vulnerable beam. 'Meacons', those cunning, deceptive radio beacons, kept plaguing the enemy bombers.

It was probably one, or perhaps more, of these snares set by the RAF's 80 Wing that led, on the night of 15 February, to a remarkable happening at Debden. With a few stray enemy aircraft about, I had been sent up to patrol. A couple of hours later the controller called men in to land — 'as soon as you can', he added, 'the weather's closing in'. Once I was down he telephoned me at the dispersal point: 'It doesn't look as if there will be any more "trade" tonight', he said, 'and the weather's getting worse. So 85 can go to release.' That meant we were free. But 'release' or not, I invariably spent the night at the dispersal point. Except that night, when thanks to a recent dose of 'flu I felt particularly exhausted. I decided to catch up on some sleep in my room in the mess and confided the night watch to Jim Marshall and Paddy Hemingway. I bade them a peaceful night.

In my bedroom I lay back between the fresh, clean sheets, for once relaxed and without a care in my head. Towards midnight, as I tuned in my Murphy portable radio, there came to my ears the distant throb of engines. It grew closer, and the familiar note made me think 'An odd Heinkel on the way home.' Then the aircraft was overhead; the sound of its engines diminished, as it apparently came in to land. I thought again: 'Must be one of ours, lost.' Some minutes later the engines were turning at full throttle and their sound faded into the night. This time I thought: 'God bless him, he's on his way again.' After listening to the news I switched off and went to sleep.

Tim called on me early next morning. 'I suppose you know what happened last night', he said, ready to spring a big surprise. 'Yes', I replied, drowsily, robbing him of the initiative, 'a Heinkel landed.' 'How the hell did you know?' demanded Tim. I did not, for certain, but I soon found out.

Those two amiable types Jim and Paddy were watching, each with a cigarette dangling from his lips, as the aircraft approached and swept into the flare of the floodlight, which someone had obligingly ordered to be switched on. 'Gosh!' exclaimed Jim. 'It's a Whitley.' 'Don't make me laugh', retorted Paddy. 'It's a Wellington.' The aircraft taxied round and stopped, its engines still turning, outside the control tower. Out came the duty pilot, 'Ace' Hodgson, a young New Zealander. He was so zealous a pilot that I had called him 'the Ace', and the name stuck. He found himself confronted by a tall young man in unfamiliar uniform who put his hand on Ace's shoulder and addressed him in an equally strange language. Only then did Hodgson realize that the man was a German, his aircraft a Heinkel 111. The two enemy airmen then retired hurriedly in the direction from which they had come.

Four officers of the Local Defence Regiment who were responsible for guarding the airfield were watching events from the roof of the control tower. Hodgson shouted to them, 'We're covered by the rear gunner. Don't shoot!' They were anyway in no position to do so, all of them having left their revolvers in their bedrooms. It was related that the 'airman of the watch' climbed into the Heinkel and asked the pilot if he needed refuelling. If that was indeed the case the German pilot was chivalrous enough to allow him to get out before he taxied back to the runway and took off.

I was rent with chagrin and frustration on hearing the full

story. Here we were, trying vainly for the last four months to shoot down a German night-bomber, and we failed to capture this one alive. It only needed someone to park a car, an ambulance or a fire tender in front of the Heinkel. But it is easy to be wise . . .

Early the following morning Leutnant Florian, pilot of another enemy bomber (a Ju 88) and his crew were flying home after bombing Liverpool when, thanks to faulty D/F bearings, they lost themselves completely. The Leutnant landed at Steeple Morden, in Bedfordshire, where he, his crew and their Ju 88 were captured.

21

THE ENEMY CAMP

The Luftwaffe bomber crews were becoming more and more aware of the dangers facing them in the night skies over Britain. The ceaseless interference with their radio beams was disconcerting enough, but that was far from being the end of their troubles. British AA fire was more intense and accurate than ever, and particularly unpleasant now that the guns (thanks to their radar 'GL') were firing unaided by searchlights and their shells bursting without warning in the dark, and dangerously close. Searchlights were no more the helpful beacons by which the Luftwaffe could identify the target. They were more powerful, more numerous and (thanks to their radar 'SLC') remarkably accurate, working in groups of six and forming a cone — remarkably efficient, the Germans found to their discomfort.

Balloons (and their cables) were a real if less frequent menace, particularly to the Luftwaffe mine-layers whose favourite waters were Plymouth harbour, the Thames, the Firth of Forth and the Mersey. Gliding down through the barrage to drop mines was a nerve-shattering experience, which the mine-layers did not always survive. One of them, a Heinkel, hit a cable and was blown to pieces by its own mine.

Although our night-fighters had not yet made any marked impact on the Luftwaffe, their bomber crews had sometimes sighted us and knew we were searching for them. The news that was getting back to them of our occasional successes was beginning to make them jumpy, to the point where one crew-member confessed that on each mission he felt obsessed by the fear of night-fighters. His problem at present was largely psychological.

When, having run the gauntlet of these several hazards, the bomber crews returned safely to base their aircraft were still not entirely secure. Sabotage of German aircraft was on the increase, and had caused some crashes. Telephone lines were another target for the saboteurs — even little boys on their way to school, a pair of tweezers in their trouser pocket, were tempted to commit such villainous crimes against the Reich.

But the morale of the young night-bomber crews, mostly in their early twenties, was high. Hitler had declared that there were no more islands, and they felt buoyed up by the certainty of invasion, come springtime. What made them believe that? 'Hitler has said so,' was the invariable answer. It was the answer I got from prisoner of war Werner Schulz when I talked to him back in May 1940 on a south-bound train from Scotland. 'The war will be over by Christmas,' he told me with a confident smile. 'What makes you think so?' I asked him, and he replied, still smiling, 'Our Fuehrer has told us.' The Fuehrer had proved to be a false prophet — not for the last time — and the older hands were feeling less confident; the air–sea blockade was not having the desired effect, U-boats were too few and British industry seemed unexpectedly resilient to the night-bombing offensive. It was when Luftwaffe prisoners were driven across London on their way to the RAF interrogation centre at Cockfosters that they received their most brutal shock: they could not believe that they were really in London. Dr Goebbels's propaganda had assured them that every window was shattered and the city in ruins. Ruins in plenty there were, of course, but London was then the biggest of all cities, and the Luftwaffe men, to their bitter disillusionment — for their efforts by day and night had been very considerable — made their own discovery that business went on as usual, with shops and theatres open and taxis and red buses plying the streets. It was not like that in Berlin, and they were worried lest Berliners might not stand up to the kind of punishment that the Luftwaffe had dealt out to London.

For the aircrews who made it back to base there were, however, certain compensations. They thought — unkindly, for they were overwrought, and living from day to day — that the only good things in France were food, champagne and public brothels. There was also other compensation in plenty, in the form of decorations which to keep up the spirits of the men, both air and ground-crew, were dispensed with a lavish hand — so lavish in fact that jokes were going round. While the Iron Cross, 2nd Class, was highly prized by the young, the older hands despised it. Everyone, they said, was bound to receive one, sooner or later, with the rations. The Iron Cross, 1st Class, however, was rightly respected. And yet there were odd cases like that of a certain *feldwebel*. On watch at a dummy airfield one night, he waited until the RAF were overhead, whereupon he took a lantern and ran here and there, hoping to attract the *Engländer bomber*. But since the wary RAF bombers refused to be tempted, the valiant *feldwebel*, so the story ended, was still running. This astonishing act of devotion earned him the Iron Cross, 1st Class.

Petty conflicts between Luftwaffe senior commanders and Göring, whom they considered (rightly) more of a politician than an airman, were often provoked by Göring himself. Dashing from base to base as fast as his bulk would allow, he delivered pep talks and bestowed medals upon all and sundry. This naturally annoyed the commanders in question, and none more than Hugo Sperrle, the massive general commanding Luftlotte 3, which operated at night over Britain. Between Göring and Sperrle it was well known that there was little love lost. After Göring had paid a surprise morale-raising visit to one of Sperrle's bases, distributing Iron Crosses, Sperrle himself arrived next day. Not to be outdone by the Reichsmarschall, he promoted nearly everyone to unteroffizier, including one man whom Göring had raised to feldwebel, a superior rank, the day before. Thank God that, in this bloody and bitter struggle, on one side and the other there was occasionally something to make us laugh.

22

CRY HAVOC!

At Debden one morning early in February I had watched as a clean-lined, mid-wing, twin-engined monoplane landed on its tricycle undercarriage. That was its most striking feature; instead of a tail wheel at the end of the fuselage there was a nose-wheel at the front. It was the first Havoc I had ever seen — not for our own keeping, but a demonstration model. And what a demonstration! Its pilot, Squadron Leader Salter, took me for a ride during which he proved that the Havoc could perform the rolls, loops and stalled turns which were the normal repertoire of a single-seater fighter. While night-fighting did not call for such antics, the Havoc's behaviour was encouraging. Not one of us, except James Wheeler, had ever flown a twin-engined aircraft. Salter further cheered us by saying how much easier it was to land with a tricycle undercarriage than to make a 'three-pricker' with the conventional landing-wheels.

Hardly had Salter left when a technical officer arrived to lecture us on the mysteries of AI, and the technique of night interception controlled by GCI. Though much diligent practice was needed to master it, the system was quite straightforward. The night-fighter was 'scrambled' under the directions of the sector controller, who then handed it over to the GCI controller. If he was already busy guiding a preceding fighter to intercept, the following one was kept waiting in the 'cab-rank'. The GCI controller called him when the next 'customer' (from the Luft-waffe) showed up, and guided him to within AI range — a few miles. Then 'Flash your weapon' the controller would order, and the night-fighter's radar operator would take over, guiding his pilot to approach the 'customer' from astern. If all went well the moment came when the pilot announced, 'O.K., I can see it.' The rest was up to him.

The technical officer had only just departed when next day Sammy Allard and his pilots of A flight hurried north to Church Fenton, there to do a short conversion course on to 'twins' — Blenheims, as it happened.

Meanwhile our first Havoc was delivered, but no one yet dared touch it. On Sammy's return I sped myself to Church Fenton to be 'converted' — by no less a person than Group Captain George Stainforth, who in a Schneider Cup Supermarine S.6 (forerunner of the Spitfire) had in the early thirties exceeded 400 mph; he was one of my boyhood heroes. In the hands of such a master, and despite my instinctive dislike of twins, I was quickly converted. After twenty minutes' solo on a Blenheim I was heading south again for Debden, there to find that a second Havoc had arrived. Still no one took to flying it, the reason being that the electricians were fitting and testing the AI and the armourers were busy on the guns — eight Brownings mounted in the nose-cockpit, which was destined, in the original bomber version, for the bomb-aimer. In the roof of his cockpit was an escape hatch, which for our pur-poses could be removed for inspection of the guns.

The look of the Havoc pleased me. After admiring it I climbed up into the cockpit. What a change from the Hurricane's cramped, uncomfortable interior! The floor of the Havoc's cock-pit was neatly laid with a green carpet and the knobs of different levers — throttle, airscrew pitch and mixture — were variously coloured in green, red and yellow. What luxury! Only one thing disturbed me — the tips of the propeller blades whirled round within a few inches of the pilot's ears. Climbing into an aeroplane cockpit was one thing; getting out — in a hurry — was quite another problem. I did not fancy the prospect of bailing out of a Havoc.

While the armourers worked on the guns, the electricians on the AI and radio, installing, adjusting, testing and making them ready for the next phase of the battle, we kept plugging away, patrolling in our Hurricanes, only too conscious that they were nearing the end of their career with us. The plane had been distinguished enough by day, but by night dogged by failure and disaster. We owed our casualties to the weather, not to the enemy, and had inflicted none on him. However,

> The heights by great men reached and kept
>   Were not attained by sudden flight,
> But they, while their companions slept,
>   Were toiling upward in the night.

On the night of 25 February I took off on patrol from Debden and climbed up beneath the black dome of the moonless sky. Visibility was good. The sector controller gave me a vector of 090° — due east — and told me to go over to 'Channel B' — the GCI frequency. Pressing the second of the four little red buttons on the control box at the left of the dashboard, I called the GCI controller. He put me to 'orbit' (circle) at 12,000 feet above the balloon barrage at Harwich.

A quarter of an hour before I left Debden a Dornier 17 of KG2, U5 + PM, had taken off from Merville — incidentally, 85 Squadron's base during the Battle of France. At the controls was 21-year-old Leutnant Heinz Patscheider, the youngest of the crew. His wireless operator, Unteroffizier Paul Schmidt, was only two years older. The veterans of the crew were Feldwebel August Beysiegel, the 27-year-old air-gunner, and the observer, Oberfeldwebel Martin Mummer. He was twenty-eight, and before joining the Luftwaffe in 1936 had worked first as a hairdresser, then as a policeman. That night of the 25th he was making his 51st flight over Britain. On this particular mission the Dornier carried sixteen 50 kg high-explosive bombs and a quantity of incendiaries. The crew had orders to attack our nightfighter airfields.

After crossing the French coast at 6000 feet, they continued climbing across the North Sea until at 12,000 feet they made a landfall just south of Harwich, where I had been circling patiently for half an hour before receiving the order 'Vector two-one-zero' — south south-west. That was the last I heard from the controller, although he was yet to hear more from me. After some minutes on a course of 210 degrees the piercing silver-blue shafts of nine searchlights suddenly shot up into the sky, and there, in the apex of their cone, glistened an aircraft steering east — too far away to identify, but I gave the Tally Ho! (aircraft sighted) to the controller and veered east at full throttle in pursuit. Before I could close with it it reached the coast and made out to sea. The searchlights groped after it, lost it and doused, leaving me peering into the dark and cursing the ill-fortune which had always been our lot. The crew of U5 + PM were at the same time cursing the British searchlights from which they had just escaped. They decided on a ruse which, they hoped, would deceive the searchlight crews into taking them for a 'friendly'.

A moment later I sighted the two navigation lights of an aircraft coming towards me. 'Suspecting trickery' (as I later recorded in my combat report), I turned in towards it. The moment it recrossed the coast the searchlights once more pierced the darkness and held it. I closed in, taking care to remain concealed from their beams, and began to stalk the mysterious plane. The dazzling glare of the light cast shadows on it, making identification difficult. To see better, I flung back the hood, but the blast of the slipstream loosened the friction buckle on the chin strap of my helmet, and the controller's voice was drowned in the bluster of the engine. I kept the hood open, for I had to be sure that the aircraft was not 'one of ours'. There had been tragic cases of mistaken identity. At first I took it for a Ju 88, with its long engine cowlings. Then, still carefully avoiding the searchlights, I slipped past astern and saw it had twin rudders. A Dornier 17? Or conceivably one of our Hampdens? If so, it had no right to be burning its navigation lights above 5000 feet. But there were foreign pilots flying with us who sometimes disregarded the rules. I moved out to the left, and it was then that I saw, unmistakable on the side of the fuselage, the black German cross. The plane was a Dornier 17. Together we had covered a lot of ground, they with their navigation lights on, cruising blithely along in the searchlights, I lurking in the surrounding shadows.

The rest happened quickly. Coming in from their left and slightly above, and still concealed from the searchlights, I held on until the last moment, then pressed the firing button. A short burst — thirty rounds — and it was over. The effect of the De Wilde was terrible; the Dornier's controls were hit, its incendiaries set on fire. Still held fast by the searchlights, the span of its wing-tips marked by its red and green navigation lights, it spiralled steeply earthward, streaming smoke and sparks, the air gunner adding to the fireworks as he poured tracers wildly into the dark. Then the stricken aircraft reared up steeply, followed by the tenacious searchlights, until as it seemed to be poised motionless at the apex of their beams there streamed from it three parachutes. I waited hopefully for the fourth, but Paul Schmidt's parachute got entangled on the tail-plane and was torn to shreds. Down went the Dornier again in a steep spiral, to crash with its load of bombs and its navigation lights still burning, near Sudbury, in Suffolk. I saw a great explosion and flames. Then — surprisingly — a stick of exploding bombs which fell across the fire. A following Luftwaffe bomber had mistaken it for a burning English target.

The Home Guard soon rounded up the Dornier's crew, Patscheider with a broken leg, Beysiegel and Mummer unhurt. The body of Paul Schmidt was discovered not far away. I felt sorry, and still do, that he had to die so young.

The combat was 85 Squadron's first — and last — night victory in Hurricanes. I owed it jointly to my comrades, pilots and ground-crew, who had never once flinched before the cruel elements, the disappointments and dangers which had been our lot. As fate would have it, I was appointed the executioner, and as such I am glad that three of my victims were reprieved at the last moment.

Neither we nor the Germans could ever be certain of our lease of life. Fate without warning could foreclose it. Faith is a surer companion than Fate, with her unpredictable caprices. Three nights after the Dornier she played me a curious trick.

It was towards midnight that I took off in my Hurricane on patrol. The controller vectored me northward, here and there, round and round, in pursuit of an elusive enemy aircraft. The weather, already doubtful, was steadily deteriorating, but it was not primarily to the elements that I owed my embarrassment that night. After an hour without the foggiest idea of my position, I called for a fix. No answer. I called and called again; still silence. The cockpit lights, I realized, were fading — I pressed the switch of the navigation lights, but neither red nor green showed up at my wing-tips. Fearing the worst, I tapped a letter or two on the Morse key to try the downward signalling lamp; it made not the faintest blink. The battery was flat. I could neither speak nor show myself to anyone, nor could anyone communicate with me. Circling, I peered down into the murk below, but could see not the slightest helpful sign or feature, beacon or coastline, below. Visually and audibly, I was cut off from the earth. The only way to return — safely or not, I could not tell — was to bail out. I steered west away from the sea for ten minutes to gain a reasonable chance of falling on dry land, and made ready to go over the side. It was only then that a strange white light, diffused by the cloud and haze, shone far below. In a moment it was gone; then it reappeared, and I dived towards it. Out it went again. When it next appeared I was clear of the drifting cloud and saw a pair of navigation lights approaching it, and another pair or two circling above. There was an airfield below, with aircraft waiting to land, which was what I wanted to do so much myself. With no lights or radio to identify myself, I could only choose a convenient aircraft, slip in behind it and follow it down to land in its wake, praying that the floodlight would shine on till I touched down. It did, and I taxied back to it. A man ran forward and climbed up to the cockpit. 'Sorry', I shouted to him, 'I'm in trouble. I'm from 85 Squadron.' 'We'll see about that,' he shouted back, thrusting a pistol into my back. 'Taxi back to the tarmac', which I did, while he still jabbed me with his pistol. I could hardly blame him, after our adventure with the Debden

Heinkel, for his unfriendly welcome. My Hurricane was no positive proof that I was British; many had been captured by the Germans in France. But in the silence which followed after the engine was switched off, when he could hear my English voice, he became more affable and I soon proved my identity. I discovered that I had landed at Langham, in Rutlandshire, 60 miles from Debden.

I flew back to Debden next day, thankful to have survived yet another brush with death. I did not believe in Fate, despite the tricks, some of them subtle, that she seemed to play on us. I ascribed these inexplicable happenings, were they good or bad for my personal well-being, to God. In those dangerous times there were few airmen, if they possessed any feeling, who did not feel an awareness of God, or whatever else they liked to call that power beyond our understanding. Many call it Fate, who at least passed for a woman. But to bow to Fate and attribute all happenings to her seemed to me too abjectly submissive. Rather than trust in Fate I preferred to believe in God. That required Faith, a challenge which put one to the test, for in our simple terms it meant courage, tenacity, morale — positive qualities — as well as resignation to cruel adversity. When after my return to Debden I landed that night from patrol in driving rain and nil visibility, I felt it more proper to thank God (yet again) rather than to congratulate myself.

March was a stern and testing month during which we worked zealously to achieve the status of specialized night-fighters. Yet we were to taste once more the bitterness of grief. Continued and uneventful night patrols in Hurricanes only spurred us to greater efforts by day in Havocs — powerful yet docile aircraft which our pilots quickly learned to handle. More and more Havocs were arriving, thanks to James Wheeler's tireless commuting between Debden and the aircraft depôt at Burtonwood, near Liverpool. A specialist radar officer, Pilot Officer Cordingley, a soft-spoken and ingenious university graduate, was appointed to our squadron. Radar operators arrived in a steady flow to be teamed up with one or other of our pilots. The one who came to me was George Barker, just commissioned, of short and solid build and an incorrigible joker. He was just my man, for over-sensitive and solemn as I may have been, I was quickly transformed when others made me laugh. There were not all that many who did, but George was one. I was glad to have him as a joker, and he produced some of his best in the most precarious situations. Joking apart, he was a highly skilled professional.

Another amiable joker was Charles Maton, who had faithfully served Sir Abe, James Bailey's father, as private secretary. He was not paired with young James — as well, maybe, for there was an age gap. Charles joined the veteran James — Wheeler — and never had we a more light-hearted yet competent team, who kept us in high spirits and embellished our reputation.

The ground crews worked like beavers during these days, for the Havoc, like all new aircraft, was plagued by teething troubles and lack of spares, to the point where our excellent technical chief, Warrant Officer Stammers, was forced to cannibalize one or two aircraft, robbing them of parts to keep the others flying. Although my personal aircraft was never decorated with any device other than the squadron and individual markings VY-Ø and the squadron's white hexagon (whose unknown origin dated from the first war), some pilots began naming their aircraft now that there was more room available on the front of the fuselage. One day in a dark corner of the hangar I noticed a dilapidated Havoc, from which most of its working parts had been removed. The broad white letters of its proud name, 'QUEEN OF THE AIR', had been scratched out and below it in chalk was scrawled 'BITCH OF THE DECK'.

One disquieting defect of the Havoc's instrumental panel was the inaccuracy of the petrol gauges — main tanks and reserve. Returning one morning after a practice flight with George, I dived down to take a close look at the dummy airfield, planted with wooden stakes and other obstructions, near to Debden. As we skimmed over it at 'nought feet' both engines cut dead. 'Now what are you going to do?' I heard George chuckling on the inter-com. My hand was already on the fuel cock, twisting it so violently on to 'Reserve' that I nearly broke my wrist. Our surplus speed from the dive gave the engines, after a few embarrassed coughs, time to pick up. George was still laughing. 'We nearly had it that time,' he called over the intercom.

Our AI–GCI interception training was in full swing, with one Havoc acting as target, the other, working with the GCI, as defending fighter, when it was decreed that these exercises should continue under the supervision of the experts at Catterick, in Yorkshire. At the prospect of quitting — if only temporarily — the warm and lively ambience of Debden, and wasting time in the process, I flew north to Catterick on the morning of the 13th to protest and plead. Shortly after lunch a mess waiter called me to the telephone. It was Tim, at Debden. 'I'm sorry; I have bad news,' he began. 'Sam Allard, the Ace and Walker-Smith have just been killed in an accident.' Shattered, I returned forthwith to Debden.

A squadron commander was obliged to make a formal report on every accident. I talked to the few witnesses available, and gathered that Sammy was to fly to Ford, in Sussex, there to collect a Havoc from 23 Squadron. Sergeant Walker-Smith accompanied him, to fly the new Havoc back to Debden. The Ace had begged Sammy to take him along for the ride — there was just room for two in the rear cockpit. An armourer told me that after loading and checking the guns he had trouble fitting the inspection panel on top of the fuselage back into place. Sammy said 'Let me help', and between them they succeeded, as far as they could tell, in securing the panel. The other vital witness was a gunner of the airfield defence manning a machine-gun at the windward end of the runway. As the Havoc roared low over his head on take-off he noticed a black object fly from the aircraft, but did not see it fall to the ground. He watched horrified as the Havoc, after a steep, short climb, stalled and went into a spin.

I inspected the wreckage — a chore I hated, but was compelled to do. The only recognizable part of the Havoc was its tail-unit; and on the leading edge of the fin were two slight dents, two feet apart, which intrigued me. Searching further, I came upon the gun-inspection panel. I picked it up and walked back to the tail-unit. It fitted exactly the two dents on the fin. It had evidently become detached and, by a chance in a million, come to rest balanced exactly across the tail-fin. Its resistance, with the engines at full power, had forced the tail down, and put the Havoc into an uncontrollable climb until it stalled and spun into the ground. Most of us, Sammy, the Ace and Walker-Smith included, had often had occasion to thank God for deliverance. Now in our immense chagrin at their death it was hard to understand his mysterious ways.

Sympathy, at once heartfelt and practical, was immediately forthcoming from our commander-in-chief, Sholto Douglas, and our group commander, Leigh-Mallory. 'L-M' informed me that the squadron was released to complete its day and night training on Havocs. How long would it take us, L-M asked, to become operational on the new type? I promised we would be ready for the night of 7 April. That would give us three weeks — precious little considering the vagaries of the weather and the dearth of spare parts. Our rehearsals for the opening night increased in tempo, especially with the technique of GCI – AI interceptions. We had flown our last night patrols on Hurricanes. We missed them, of course, and although our contribution to the night defence of the realm had been practically negligible, it was now non-existent — just at the moment when the Luftwaffe resumed in earnest its night offensive against our island.

Luftwaffe strategy being to complement the U-boat blockade, their renewed and savage attacks were directed mainly against our ports. The first to suffer was Cardiff, at the beginning of March. London's turn came next, when on each of the nights of the 8th and 9th, 150 bombers were over the docks and city and the dead in London were numbered in hundreds. Hundreds more civilians died when Portsmouth, Plymouth, Bristol, Liverpool, Glasgow and Hull were all sorely hit with high explosive and incendiaries. Nor, in the industrial Midlands, were Birmingham and Coventry spared. Inevitably it was again London's turn. A sharp attack on the night of 15 March was the prelude to a mass assault by nearly 500 bombers on the 19th which left 751 Londoners dead and hundreds more badly injured — a massacre not of the British plutocracy whom

Göring had bombastically claimed was his target but of the poorer folk of the east and south-east of London.

Woolwich took heavy punishment. In the Arsenal, stores and workshops were demolished and set ablaze. To the south, where the ground rises towards the Common, military barracks — the Cambridge, Connaught and Grand Depôt, known to many an earlier generation of the Army, were shattered, as well as the lives of scores of young soldiers within their walls.

Less than fifty yards away, Mulgrave Road School, hit by oil bombs, went up in flames. Not that this caused much sorrow to Ray Callow, who had been evacuated there after his own school, Burrage Grove, had been hit. But Ray, home from duty in the Town Hall, that night witnessed a sight which brought such horror to his young eyes that he still remembers it vividly. A heavy bomb damaged a house in Eaton Road, not more than thirty yards from the Callow home, where soldiers back on leave were chatting and playing cards with friends. Rescue squads found six of them dead, without a scratch on them. Blast had snuffed out their lives. A seventh, an elderly lady, had been killed by flying debris. Ray was watching when stretcher-men carried her body out. They rolled it off the stretcher and tipped it into a kind of all-purpose metal coffin; Ray caught a fleeting glimpse of the dead woman's face, the mangled features, the hair clotted with blood and brick dust. That was the most awful sight ever engraved on the mind of young Ray.

At the AFS sub-station at Earldom Square the girl operator pushed down two bells: 'Numbers one and two pumps, Lewisham!' Many pumps had already reached the blaze when Johnny's number one pump and Steve Needham's number two reached the unimaginable shambles — scattered and burning wares from market stalls, from clothes shops, grocers, fruiterers, toyshops and the rest. Charred remnants of fruit and vegetables, clothes, boots, smashed dolls and smouldering teddy bears lay strewn everywhere. For two and a half hours Johnny and his men helped fight the blaze while the chief fire officer directed operations, shouting orders: 'Numbers one, two and five in there, then out and across to the right . . .' Walking backward with an eye on the pumps as they moved with the flames, the chief fire officer had just shouted, 'Now you, get in there!' when his voice fell silent. He had 'got in' himself, into a bomb crater full of muddy water. As he crawled out, dripping from his tin hat downward, the firemen dared not laugh — not until they were on their way back to the sub-station.

The Luftwaffe immediately followed up that slaughter of London's poor with a heavy two nights' attack on Plymouth's dockland, Devonport. There came a lull of two weeks ending in early April with more violent assaults on the west-coast ports, Bristol, Liverpool and Glasgow, at the receiving end of Britain's Atlantic lifeline. Then as a change from mauling our ports and their stubborn, unconquerable people nearly 250 Luftwaffe bombers flew off into the night of 8 April to hammer Coventry, whose people as ever had no more intention than any other citizens in the land of bowing before the would-be conqueror.

On their side, the would-be conquerors and notably the Luftwaffe — seriously disturbed by their failure to crush British morale, blockade British ports and destroy British industry — were having a hard think about improving their methods. The problems facing them were accumulating night by night. To begin with the German aircrews found the blackout over Britain embarrassingly effective — all but those red flashing beacons which showed us the way to go home but continued to puzzle the enemy.

Then there were decoy fires, 'Starfish', the creation of Colonel Turner. German observers had their own pet ones, and were extremely wary of them. It was when decoy fires appeared to be part of the target that they looked like any other blaze, well worthy of a stick of bombs. When isolated they deceived no one; they had an unreal look, too compact, the flames too yellow instead of the lurid red of a real blaze belching smoke. A rumour spread among the Luftwaffe that shortage of firewood was forcing the British to give up decoy fires. There they were over-hasty; Starfish were yet to fool the Luftwaffe and collect many more bombs destined for vital targets.

The blackout, Starfish sites and red flashing beacons were

relatively minor worries compared with the failure, thanks to 'Aspirin' jammers, of Knickebein to guide the Luftwaffe bombers to their targets. At this check to his favourite gadget Göring fumed, venting his anger on his unfortunate *Gruppe Kapitänen*. Yet it was none of their fault. Göring should have sent a rude letter to the erudite Dr Cockburn, inventor of 'Aspirin'. Cockburn's 'Bromide' jammer, though increasingly successful against the X-Gerät of Kampfgruppe 100, had not yet put an end to their fire-raising pathfinder activities. Crack unit as it had always been in navigation, its crews in broad moonlight were able to identify and mark their target with precision. As for Y-Gerät, the specialist unit, 3/KG26, were so bothered by Cockburn's 'Domino' jammer that out of 89 raids, it fuddled them completely in all but eighteen. Accumulating gradually too were the successes of British night-fighters and AA guns. Their results, if modest and still perhaps more psychological than material, were regular, night after night.

It was not easy for the Luftwaffe to remount or intensify its offensive. One factor might have tipped the balance against the British: a four-engined bomber. Göring, with characteristic lack of foresight, had rejected the idea in the mid-thirties. Since then the four-engined Focke-Wulf 200 (or Kondor) had been built, and with its long range and reliability was plaguing our Atlantic convoys. But it did not threaten Britain as a long-range bomber. Only now was the four-engined, twin-propeller Heinkel 177 coming into production. It could carry two 'Max' 2500 kg bombs. It was still full of bugs, and anyway was conceived, like the Focke-Wulf 200, primarily for reconnaissance and only extreme long-range bombing.

Meanwhile the Luftwaffe confined themselves to tactical considerations: London was best approached from the west, with the Thames, the Serpentine, parks and railway termini as landmarks — much more peaceful than from the east, following the Thames estuary, where AA was thick on the ground. With night-bombing so inaccurate, raids were to be concentrated during the period of the bombers' moon to give the best possible chance of target identification and accurate aiming. The bomber should approach 'up-moon', more easily to identify the target by its silhouette or its reflection on water. But there was a danger: the bomber itself would be clearly silhouetted, for the benefit of the night-fighter which might be on its tail.

There was a funny idea in the minds of some Luftwaffe night-bomber aircrew that British night-fighter pilots were drawn from owners of sports cars. It is true, in my own case, that I owned an MG in Singapore in 1936 and a sporty little Standard with wire wheels a few years later, but my present model was a solid Rover 10 saloon. RAF 'types' were generally fond of sports cars, but night-fighter pilots did not possess a monopoly. The respect for our night-fighters was growing, whether it was because of our supposed preference for sports cars or our growing profes-sionalism as night-fighters. Luftwaffe crews were now beating it for home at 5000 feet, well below our normal patrol heights, in the hope of avoiding us.

They were arming themselves, too, with peculiar devices, with the intention of discouraging our unwanted attention: things like a towed kite, or jets of petrol which ignited automatically, or grenades pushed down a chute at the bottom of which was a trigger which fired them — and God help the bomber if the grenade got stuck at the bottom of the chute, where it was sure to explode prematurely. As for the front end of the bomber: one in every *Staffel* was now being fitted with an improved balloon-cutting device, a pole which projected, like the horn of a narwhal, from the end of which a wire extended to each wing-tip where a small explosive charge would sever any balloon cable deflected in its direction. Aerial balloon-sweeping was to be con-fided to one unlucky crew in each *Staffel* who would clear the way for the following aircraft. The tactic looked unlikely to be a great success. Finally, the most sensible idea of all was a system to boost the speed of a bomber in emergency: gas or compressed air was fed into the supercharger, enabling the aircraft to make a sudden spurt and leave the pursuing fighter standing. For this reason, perhaps, the system was called Ha-ha. These were some of the bright ideas of the German boffins which, like those of our own, were seldom put into practice.

The spirits of the Luftwaffe bomber crews were high, buoyed up as they were by hopes of the coming invasion of Britain and by letters from their loved ones in Germany which told of increasing movement and ferment in the Fatherland with the approach of spring. Rumours were circulating of a new 'secret weapon', the *Seilbombe*, a sort of kite loaded with explosive and designed to be towed behind low-flying aircraft for the purpose of cutting high-tension cables and telephone wires in Britain. With all this invasion fever went a sincere if mistaken belief in the 'humanity' of the Fuehrer, Adolf Hitler, ridiculed though he was on the British side. Germans believed that Hitler, onetime corporal in the German Imperial Army, knew the horrors of war so well that he wished to spare his country yet more suffering. An admirable sentiment, were it true. But it was not. Hitler was only too ready to sacrifice the lives of German soldiers, sailors and airmen, of their families and sweethearts, to his ambition of becoming master of Europe, perhaps of the world.

The Luftwaffe lost a hundred men over Britain during March. That did not discourage them. On the contrary, a more insidious influence was creeping into their hearts, tending to weaken their will to fight. Quite simply, it was the easy life that they enjoyed at their bases in France, good lying, good living with plentiful food and wine and girls. Few were the French girls who consented, but there was no lack of German girls serving like our WAAFs, in the Luftwaffe. They were nicknamed *Blitzmädchen*, were aged between eighteen and thirty-five and working as telephonists and radio operators — cheerful girls, conscientious, intelligent and discreet.

Naturally, Paris was the big attraction for all, but serious restrictions opposed a visit to the City of Light. Only soldiers and civilians with urgent reasons were considered. A permit was needed for the person and his car. Luftwaffe men had to report to the Provost Marshal of the Luftwaffe at 62 rue du Faubourg Saint-Honoré, where they were allotted permits and lodgings. The curfew fell for NCOs at 11 p.m., for officers at midnight. Regulation dress was required, 'fully buttoned up'. Luftwaffe men could travel free on the Métro, first class where it applied.

THE AFTERMATH

The area around St Paul's was laid waste in the Blitz – yet despite a bomb which fell into the crypt, damaging the High Altar on the way, the cathedral itself remained largely intact and an inspiring symbol of the endurance of the British people.

Above: Londoners walk along a narrow pathway between bombed buildings in Goswell Road, E1, after one of the worst night attacks of the Second World War – 29 December 1940. *Associated Press*

Below: St Paul's Cathedral. Fallen masonry on the High Altar and a hole in the east roof caused by a high explosive bomb. 6 am, 10 October 1940. *Guildhall Library*

Below: The crypt can be glimpsed through the bomb crater in the cathedral floor. *Guildhall Library*

Above: A view from the cathedral roof looking over the ruined city towards Paternoster Row. *Guildhall Library*

Below: Madame Tussaud's, Marylebone Road, NW1, 9 September 1940. Many waxwork were lost. *BBC Hulton Picture Library*

reet scene, Balham, London, 17 October 1940. (Note the ironic sign on the right.) *BBC* *ulton Picture Library*

Above: The historic Guildhall in the City after a night raid, 29 December 1940. The giant mythological figures of Gog and Magog were lost in the debris of the Great Hall. (A crown belonging to one of the figures can be seen in the centre of the picture.) Monuments to Wellington, Nelson, Pitt and Chatham were among those damaged. *Guildhall Library*

Above: Among the many beautiful Wren churches destroyed in the London Blitz was St Mary Le Bow, Cheapside. Originally burnt down in the Great Fire of London, 1666, it was subsequently rebuilt by Sir Christopher Wren c. 1680. The church was gutted in a night raid on 8 December 1940. (It has now been restored.) New 'Bow Bells' were recast from those damaged in the Blitz. *Guildhall Library*

Below: Liverpool Street Station, London, damaged by two high explosive bombs (January 1941) which exploded simultaneously at Nos 135 and 151 Bishopsgate at 8.20 pm, causing approximately 60 casualties, of which 38 were fatal. *Guildhall Library*

Above: Damage in the West End looking down Piccadilly from the Circus (with Eros removed for safety throughout the war), 14 October 1940. *Associated Press*

Below: Central Criminal Court ('Old Bailey'), EC4. Barristers' entrance. High Explosive bomb, 10 May 1941. *Guildhall Library*

Below: Churchill surveys the damage at the House of Commons, Palace of Westminster, SW1, May 1941. *Popperfoto*

LIFE GOES ON . . .

Throughout the Blitz, the inhabitants of London and provincial cities went about their daily tasks much as usual, and shops, offices and theatres remained open. Hitler and the Luftwaffe's inability to break the morale of the British people was one of the factors which brought about an eventual cessation of the bombing.

Above: Shoppers buy bread from a damaged bakery in an area bombed earlier that day, 23 August 1940. *Associated Press*

Above: A couple bombed out of their home pile their belongings onto a pram – with a black kitten for luck. 15 September 1940. *Associated Press*

Below: King George VI and Queen Elizabeth inspect bomb damage at Colindale Avenue, Hendon, 27 September 1940. *Associated Press*

above: Londoners sleeping in the tube during a night raid, 27 September 1940. (By 1941 London Underground stations had bunks for 725,000 civilians.) *Associated Press*

Below: Miss Ellen Wilkinson, Parliamentary Secretary to the Ministry for Home Security, photographed with some of the children in a London tube station shelter during a tour of inspection. 10 October 1940. *Associated Press*

Below: Suburban homes on the outskirts of London the morning after a raid. (Censorship prevented the exact location being indicated on many wartime photographs.) *BBC Hulton Picture Library*

Above: Despite the presence of a huge bomb crater, passers-by still feed the pigeons as usual in Trafalgar Square. 13 October 1940. *Associated Press*

Left: An Eastender at his bombed house, 28 September 1940. *BBC Hulton Picture Library*

But they had orders to keep aloof from French civilians; they were prohibited from dancing, from smoking in the streets, on the Métro and in buses, from sitting on bar stools in public places. It was also forbidden to allow Frenchwomen to ride in Service cars, and to walk arm-in-arm with the opposite sex. Good manners were required in every situation, and soldierly bearing.

Such were the enemy, the young men we were fighting. But they were not always so restrained as their code of discipline might suggest. Some who fell on our side told of the fantastic orgies they had enjoyed. Others, less fortunate, whose mutilated bodies were washed up on our shores, had in their pockets French money, tickets for the Paris Opéra, the Empire (the soldiers' theatre in the avenue Wagram), the Champs Elysées, the avenue Montaigne. They had their fun when they could get it, as we did. We occasionally spent a night at the Coconut Grove, or at Kate Meyrick's 43 Club. But London, unlike Paris, was being bombed. At least our rare visits to the city, when bad weather at the airfield permitted, enabled us to share in a small way the lot of Londoners. We amused ourselves as the bombs crashed around. When we were driving home one night a canister of incendiaries just missed the car. All that was good for us, for it helped to close the great gulf between us, patrolling miles up in the darkness, and those who were 'taking it' below.

Usually Luftwaffe crews visiting Paris put up at the Monty Hotel. Near by was the well-known Lotti, where the Gestapo were lodged, and it was a dire experience for a Luftwaffe man when the Monty was full and he had to spend the night with the Gestapo at the Lotti. Luftwaffe crews, greatly fearing the Gestapo, were at this time particularly reticent towards their RAF interrogations. Happy in the belief of a German victory, they all the same dreaded an eventual investigation by the Gestapo on their talks with their RAF interrogators.

23

BRITAIN'S STRUGGLE ON DISTANT FRONTS

The first half of 1941, Churchill recalled later, imposed more stress and brought greater problems upon himself and his colleagues than any other period during the war. Britain — still alone, and surrounded by German-held Europe, but loyally supported by the Commonwealth and aided by her great friend the United States — was fighting both the Axis powers, Germany and Italy, on several fronts. On the home front she was holding out, thanks mainly to the bravery of her citizens, against the repeated onslaughts of the Luftwaffe. Far away, on other fronts, she was striving both for survival and for conquest — in the Atlantic and the Mediterranean, in North Africa and East Africa. Meanwhile there were sinister portents of a new Axis front developing in the Balkans, with its threat for the safety of friendly Greece, and of Yugoslavia, whose friendship had yet to be proved.

Britain's own fate depended ultimately on the Battle of the Atlantic. As long as British merchantmen and those of other nations brave enough to share the perils of the cruel sea could reach British ports and discharge their cargoes of food, arms and equipment (including our Havocs), Britain could hold out indefinitely. Of that Churchill was sure, even if it came to a German invasion. That was still considered as a very present threat, but one which, as Churchill nicely put it: '. . . would not be disadvantageous to us'. Our Army, the Home Guard and our air force, both bombers and fighters, had increased immensely in strength. As for the Navy, they could always be trusted to defend the waters surrounding our island.

In the broad Atlantic and the northern approaches where they and the RAF's Coastal Command kept watch over the convoys, their task was far harder. Despite their constant vigilance, sinkings of merchant ships were, in Churchill's words, 'awe-striking'. The Kriegsmarine's U-boats were now hunting in 'wolf-packs', with more disastrous results than ever before for the convoys. Early in April a 'wolf-pack' sank ten ships out of a convoy of twenty-two. The U-boats were not alone. While the German pocket battleship *Admiral Scheer*, after five months of ravaging British convoys, had returned to Germany, the battle-cruisers *Scharnhorst* and *Gneisenau* had broken out into the North Atlantic and the heavy cruiser *Admiral Hipper* was still at large. All had had close brushes with British escorting battleships but were taking no risks. Between them, in two months, they sent twenty-two merchantmen to the bottom, often not stopping to pick up survivors. These were grievous losses, but did not go without retribution. In March five U-boats were sunk, one of them, the *U:47*, commanded by the ace Prien, and two others, *U.99* and *U.100*, by two other distinguished commanders. These were grievous losses for the enemy. Despite the appalling figures, 350,000 tons of shipping sunk, the first round of the Battle of the Atlantic had in Churchill's view ended in a draw. But it was far from over. The mid-Atlantic was the danger area, and in April Churchill was forced to admit 'Somehow we had to contrive to extend our reach, or our days were numbered.' It was then that the United States Navy came to the rescue, when President Roosevelt extended their zone of patrol eastward to the meridian 26° West, to cover more than half of their side of the Ocean. While the navy of the United States — still a non-belligerent — could provide no direct protection to British convoys, they could and did report enemy movements in their zone to the Royal Navy.

In the Mediterranean naval supremacy was essential to British plans in Greece and North Africa. Since November RAF squadrons, both fighter and bomber, had been detached from Northern Africa (where they could ill be spared) and sent to Greece. Fighting alongside the Greeks, the RAF had helped in full measure in the rout of the Italian armies. Now that it was clear to Churchill that, faced with an imminent German invasion of their country, the Greeks were going to fight to the end, he decided in early March to aid Greece more fully. The forces, ground and air, sent to Greece and Crete would have to be taken from the North African front, itself unmistakably threatened by the Germans. The transport of these reinforcements would put a further strain on our already overburdened Mediterranean fleet, heavily engaged in seeing convoys from the west and east through to Malta, the British naval base some eighty miles south of Sicily. That beleaguered island had been bombed fifty-eight times during January, and now that Luftwaffe units were based in Sicily and Pantellaria island, midway between Sicily and the north African coast, Malta was destined to be bombarded from the air in the months to come on an average of two or three times a day.

Thanks to the complaisance of Bulgaria, Romania and Hungary, German forces had been crossing those countries and massing both on the northern frontier of Greece and on the frontier of Serbia, in southern Yugoslavia. The Luftwaffe by the end of January was installed on Bulgarian airfields, within striking distance of Greece and Crete.

Yugoslavia, which could also allow access to Greece's northern frontier, was not so ready to co-operate until the Regent, Prince Paul, uncle of the young king Peter II, visited Hitler secretly in his mountain eyrie at Berchtesgaden. There the amiable Prince bowed to the German Fuehrer's desires. But Yugoslavia refused to let themselves be caught so easily in the German snare. The air force general, Simovič, supported by a band of young Serb officers, had planned a rising against the government. Prince Paul on his return was forced to abdicate; King Peter — after making good his escape by sliding down a drain-pipe — appeared at Divine Service in Belgrade cathedral on Friday 28 March, to be wildly acclaimed, while some of the crowd insulted the German minister and spat on his car. Hitler, enraged, prepared vengeance on this heroic people.

That Sunday of the revolution in Belgrade, the British Mediterranean fleet scored a signal victory against the Italian fleet off Cape Matapan, at the southern tip of Greece. Meanwhile British, Australian and New Zealand troops were taking up positions alongside the Greek army. All waited for the blow to fall.

Some hundreds of miles south across the Mediterranean, on the shores of Africa, the British Army of the Nile, with strong Australian support, was again on the move. After its brilliant victory early in January against the Italians at Bardia, its armour and infantry pushed on westward, capturing Tobruk, with 30,000 prisoners, a fortnight later. Tobruk, with its port, was a valuable prize; supplies could be carried there direct by sea instead of being off-loaded at Alexandria and forwarded along the coastal road. The British and Australians pressed on another 250 miles across the desert and on 6 February captured Benghazi, where the bearded Italian general, Bergonzoli — nicknamed 'Electric Whiskers' — surrendered. The Italian army no longer existed; it had lost 130,000 prisoners, hundreds of tanks and over a thousand guns.

As with Greece, so with North Africa. German troops were massing to fill the gap left by the Italians; they disembarked at Tripoli in Libya. The German general, Erwin Rommel — soon to earn the name of the Desert Fox — was making ready to counter-attack.

The task of General Wavell, commander-in-chief of the British in the Middle East, was one that would have daunted a lesser man. By March 1941 his armies were facing the enemy on fronts as widely dispersed as Greece, North Africa, Ethiopia and Somalia; other formations stood ready for action in Palestine and Kenya. In December 1940, after the victory at Sidi Barrani, Wavell wisely dispatched the 4th British-Indian Division to Port Sudan in anticipation of a new offensive against the Italians in their colonies of Ethiopia, Eritrea and Somalia. They arrived in time to join the 5th British-India Division in the pursuit of the enemy, who on 19 January had evacuated Kassala, in the Sudan, and were falling back eastward across the border into Ethiopia, where the British under General William Platt continued to pursue them into northern Eritrea. There, before the stronghold of Keren, some eighty miles from the Red Sea, the British were halted by obstinate Italian resistance. Platt would need time to prepare his final assault.

A thousand miles to the south, on the shores of the Indian Ocean, General Alan Cunningham, at the head of the 11th African Division and the 1st African Brigade, landed at Kismayu, in southern Somalia, in mid-February. Advancing inland his forces, supported by aircraft of the South African Air Force, overran the strongly-held position of Jelib and put the enemy to rout. Cunningham turned north-east, and three days later entered Mogadishu, Somalia's main port, 200 miles away. There, among a mass of abandoned stores, he found 400,000 gallons of petrol which helped to assure his next long leap of 740 miles across desert and hills to Jijiga, in Ethiopia, which was reached on 17 March. Cunningham's forces then veered north-west towards Harar, which surrendered on 26 March. Three days later he entered Diredawa. Since Kisamayu he had covered nearly 1000 miles of difficult terrain, and accounted for more than 50,000 of the enemy for the loss of 500 of his own men. After a pause at Diredawa to regain their breath, Cunningham's forces continued another 200 miles into the mountains towards the capital, Addis Abbaba, which they entered on 6 April.

Meanwhile before Keren, far to the north, General Platt's 4th and 5th British-Indian Divisions were ready for the assault on 15 March. Though harassed by the South African Air Force and RAF squadrons from Aden, the Italians held out stubbornly, and it was only on 27 March, at the cost of 3000 casualties, that Keren was overrun. Platt's forces pushed on immediately to the pleasant town of Asmara, which they entered on 1 April. The port of Massawa, on the Red Sea, was captured, with 10,000 prisoners, on 8 April. By this time the Italian naval force in the Red Sea had been entirely eliminated by the Royal Navy and the Fleet Air Arm. Pockets of Italian resistance in the mountains of

Ethiopia had still to be cleared up. But the days of Mussolini's new Roman Empire were numbered.

While Britain fought on with varying fortune across this immense battlefield of the Atlantic, the Mediterranean, Greece, North and East Africa and over Germany itself, it was hard not to feel that the part played by my squadron in the struggle was negligible. I often thought of my brothers — Michael on the bridge of his destroyer, fighting somewhere on the high seas, and Philip with the Gurkha Rifles in India. His fight against the Japanese was yet to come. Yet paltry by comparison as our efforts may have been, we were certainly doing our utmost to strengthen the night defences of our cities, and above all London. For the home front was paramount. If, after all the valiant struggles on other fronts, Britain yielded, her hopes of beating Hitler would collapse around her. Britain was a fortress, the only one still inviolate, from which some time in the future sallies could be made against the foe. Hitler himself (as noted by his Chief of Staff, General Halder) had in January said as much to his military chiefs: 'The British can hope to win the war only by beating us on the Continent. The Fuehrer is convinced that this is impossible.' More than three long years were yet to pass before Hitler was to discover that he was mistaken. In the meantime Britain must hold out.

24

THE HOME FRONT: THE NIGHT BATTLE APPROACHES ITS CLIMAX

On 7 April, as promised, I reported 85 Squadron at readiness for operations that night. After days and nights of training, the Squadron at last took its place alongside the specialized night-fighter squadrons — 25, 29, 68, 219, 600 and 604, all of them equipped with Beaufighters. No. 85, with its Havocs, was the ugly duckling and not quite so well off as the Beaufighters in performance and armament, let alone experience. But we were of the same metal as the rest, and only time would show how well we could do. Completing the regular night-fighter force were eight 'cats-eye' squadrons flying Hurricanes and Defiants. Given moonlight, visibility and GCI control, the 'cats-eyes' continued to inflict losses on the enemy. No. 23 'Intruder' Squadron operated over enemy territory.

I was among a few others who on the night of the 7th made their first operational patrol in a Havoc. The enemy were headed for Liverpool, and no 'trade' came our way, any more than on the night of the 8th, when the Luftwaffe attacked Coventry. The following night witnessed the beginning of a dramatic change in our fortunes. After six months of futile searching in the dark we suddenly, scientifically, that night found three enemy aircraft.

It was Geoff Howitt and his operator Sergeant Reed who won the Squadron's first victory on Havocs. A waxing moon near to full and the air as clear as crystal made for better sighting — not only for the night-fighter, but for the enemy upper and lower rear gunners on the look-out. After the GCI — call sign Cranford — had guided Geoff for some time out to sea, a good blip came up on Reed's cathode tube, and at 9000 feet he guided his pilot in from astern, when Geoff had a good 'visual' of a Heinkel 111, its crew evidently unaware of their impending fate. An excellent pilot, cool and matter-of-fact, Geoff sent a deadly stream of fire into the bomber; he could see the flashes of his De Wilde bullets as they struck home, tearing off bits of metal which flashed past dangerously close to the Havoc. The Heinkel dived steeply and crashed into the sea. One enemy aircraft destroyed.

Jim Marshall and his operator Sergeant Hallett were next off, and the GCI soon put them on the track of a 'bandit' which, after Hallett had taken over on the AI, Jim sighted in front, but a thousand feet below at an altitude of 14,000 feet. Throttling back gently to prevent the engines from streaming visible flames of late-burning gas, Jim lost height, and closed in behind his target. But the Heinkel's gunners had seen him and replied to his fire. Through streams of tracer he could see his De Wilde striking the left wing of the Heinkel. It pulled up, dived steeply and disappeared from Jim's view, and from the cathode tube. One enemy aircraft damaged.

An hour before midnight I took off with George Barker seated before his radar set. Behind him in the rear cockpit stood Sergeant Bailey, a young Australian and an airman to the bone; his father had been a crewman with the famous pioneer pilot Charles Kingsford-Smith, yet another of my boyhood heroes.

That night I had decided on an experiment, impressed as I had been by the Defiant's ability to attack with its hydraulic four-gun turret from underneath the enemy.

I had rigged up in the rear cockpit of my Havoc a Vickers 'K' machine-gun; the mounting could only take one, hand-operated at that. Bailey, a radar operator by trade, had volunteered to come with me as gunner. We climbed away into the night in great fettle, as was always the case, with George chuckling in the back seat. None of us dreamed that the joke in the end would be on us. At 14,000 feet Cranford put me on to a bandit. After some

minutes George had a blip and after a five minutes chase I
sighted a Ju 88 300 yards in front and above. I was overtaking
fast, so rather than throttle right back and risk being spotted
from my engines' exhaust flames, I made a series of S-turns
before slowly closing in from below and astern. Then, dazzled
by the diffused moonlight on my plastic 'Perspex' windscreen, I
lost sight of the bomber. George immediately took over and
soon brought me back into visual contact. As we continued to
close, all three of us saw flashes just beyond our own left wing-
tip — very probably exploding grenades, a gadget occasionally
used by the enemy. He had evidently seen us. Now very close, I
opened fire, but while George reported De Wilde strikes, my own
view was completely obscured by the blinding flashes of my eight
forward guns, while smoke and cordite fumes filled my cockpit.
As the enemy dived, turning violently left and right, I followed,
and at 11,000 feet began stalking him again. But he could still see
us, thanks to our searchlights which firmly held me, but only
occasionally flickered on him. We now came under intensive and
accurate fire. George reported hits on our right wing and engine
and more on the left wing; also that his microphone had frozen
up and he had exchanged it for Bailey's, which left him and
Bailey connected to each other like Siamese twins, and both of
them plugged into Bailey's socket. I stuck on the enemy's tail, but
during my violent evasive action to dodge his flying bullets
Bailey was floored and George unseated. However, he managed
to grab the Vickers gun and pump a few bullets into the Junkers'
belly as we finally slid below it. George — and I could still detect
his chuckle — then shouted: 'The bloody gun's jammed!' I now
gathered myself for another front-gun attack, and this time approached unobserved to within close range. When I opened fire
we all saw a mass of De Wilde strikes and a fair-size explosion in
the right engine. Then our stubborn enemy, lurching clumsily to
the right, went down in a long, steep dive until he disappeared
from both visual and radar contact. We had been trying to kill
each other for the last half-hour.

In making out my combat report I claimed the Junkers as
probably destroyed; a Junkers 88 did crash in our sector, its

survivors saying it had been repeatedly attacked by a night-fighter. But the evidence was not conclusive. Our Junkers may have fallen into the sea; bodies of Luftwaffe crews were continually being washed up on our shores. If ever it got back, then the crew would be able to spread the story that our night-fighters were around, and that they were becoming more dangerous. Psychology in war is a powerful factor. The Luftwaffe high command were becoming increasingly worried at the losses of their night bombers. The crews themselves were suffering more and more bereavements among their friends. Two and sometimes three sorties in a single night were putting crews under mounting stress, which would only be aggravated by their growing fear of British night-fighters. One unhappy young radio-operator of 3/KG 53 was so obsessed with a fear of night-fighters that, imagining his Heinkell 111 was being continually followed, he kept screaming false warnings on the intercom to his pilot. His fears were finally put to rest when the 20 mm cannon shells of a Beaufighter tore into his Heinkel and killed him.

In my own Havoc we were lucky to land intact, at about half past midnight. George had warned me of the strikes on our aircraft, but he could not tell that the oil tank of the right engine had been holed. The oil pressure held up, just, until landing. By then the oil tank was empty and the engine on the point of seizing up. The enemy gunner after raking the right wing and engine had been obliging enough to lift his gun over my cockpit before putting more bullets into the left wing. For George the biggest joke of the night, apart from his and Bailey's tangle in the rear cockpit, was the stray bullet which somehow had made its way through one leg of his trousers.

When I took off next night, the 10th of April, it was with George alone. The good Bailey, after his adventures of the night before, was in no hurry to accompany us. We all agreed that in theory the rear-gun attack from below was in certain situations a valid alternative — Defiants were still proving it — to the front-gun attack. But a single, hand-operated rear gun fired from an open cockpit was clearly not the equal of the Defiant's four-gun hydraulic turret.

My thoughts on this subject were, I believe, influenced — already — by the conviction that our eight forward-firing .303 guns were at night far from adequate. Aiming at and hitting one's target at night, even under the benign light of the moon, was far more tricky than by day. Darkness dulled the visual senses, and other reflexes as well. This considered, I had pleaded since Gravesend, four months ago, for the most lethal armament possible. The Havoc's battery of eight .303 machine-guns installed in the nose had that grave disadvantage of blinding the pilot, at least until the guns were fitted with 'flash-eliminators' — a kind of cone fitted to the end of the barrel. And it was too feeble. The Beaufighters with nearly as many machine-guns — six — plus four 20 mm cannons seldom missed. I demanded that four cannons be fitted as soon as possible. In the meantime our numerous night interceptions too often ended, for want of fire-power, in inconclusive combat.

As I took off with George just after midnight the following night — 11 April — we felt surer of ourselves as a regular crew of pilot and radar operator. George's humorous asides were as always stimulating. Vectored by Cranford on to a raid, George soon picked it up on his AI cathode tube until I sighted, above and slightly to the left, a Ju 88. It took me a few more minutes to stalk in unseen to close range. Then I opened fire, and while the reassuring flashes of my De Wilde were visible, the tongues of flame from my guns made it impossible to hold my aim through the reflector sight. I released the firing button in time to see tracer coming from the Junkers, which swung violently to the left and went down in a steep dive, streaming little jets of flame, like bright red and yellow silk handkerchiefs, until it was lost to my own visual and George's radar view. One Ju 88 damaged. A disappointing combat, for he looked a 'goner', as I wrote in my combat report 'on the way down'. I could only wish him bon voyage on the way home.

That brief affair over, I climbed up again on an indistinct vector of 330° from Cranford and heard no more from him. But from George came a sudden Tally Ho! We were close to the summit of a towering, moonlit mass of cumulus cloud. Before

George could utter another word, a Heinkel, easily recognizable, suddenly appeared from the shadows, a hundred yards away and on a converging course. We both swerved violently to avoid collision, and I grabbed the throttles back, hoping to slip in behind him. But he, understandably frightened, was already diving ahead of me into the shadowy canyon of cloud, and was quickly lost in its depths.

In mid-April came a signal concerning me personally. It informed me that I was to be posted to 11 Group Headquarters. Although the news was disappointing, I was prepared for it. I had been on active operations day and night since the war began twenty months ago, and commanding 85 Squadron for nearly a year. Moreover, I was well aware that my physical and nervous resources were running low. However, I could not accept the prospect of leaving 85 at this moment when, after all our vain searching in the dark, we were now beginning to catch the enemy night after night; and while problems nevertheless remained to be solved with the maintenance and armament of our Havocs. I hastened off to 11 Group to plead with L-M, and he — as always ready to listen — allowed me a stay of execution until mid-June, with a kindly word of advice: 'Take it easy a bit.'

During the first half of April the Luftwaffe, except for a heavy raid on Coventry, had pursued their strategy of 'strangulation' with night attacks on our ports: Liverpool and Glasgow, Bristol, Birmingham, Belfast and Tyneside. It was perhaps a heavy raid on Berlin by RAF Bomber Command, whose navigation and bomb-aiming was often praised by Luftwaffe prisoners, that provoked massive retaliation by the Germans on London. On 16 April — 'the Wednesday, as Londoners would remember it — nearly seven hundred bombers assaulted the capital, killing over a thousand of its citizens and injuring more than twice that number, besides hitting thirteen churches and eighteen hospitals. A captured German bomb-aimer when asked to describe his feelings about killing hospital patients replied: 'Well, they were already half dead, so I have no regrets.' Mass aerial bombardment of unarmed and anonymous innocents was surely the most callous and degrading of all kinds of warfare.

'The Wednesday' had seen London's most murderous raid to date, but the attack of over seven hundred bombers on 19 April, 'the Saturday', caused as much slaughter in the capital. These two horrible massacres were a measure of the continuing failure of the British night defences, despite their unrelenting efforts, to protect the civilian population. While the night-fighters for their part were inflicting increasing losses on the enemy, they were still not enough to deter him.

Leaving London to mourn its dead, the Luftwaffe turned again on our ports. Night after night through the rest of April and into May they mercilessly battered the ports on their hit-list, adding Sunderland for good measure. Thus did they hope to reduce them to rubble, and render them useless. But the people of the ports held out, and their repair and restoration services kept the docks in operation.

Our progress in 85 Squadron was encouraging — at least by comparison with the past — although it was already evident from the number of inconclusive combats that our Havocs needed more clout than their eight machine-guns, with their blinding flash, could provide. On that Wednesday night, guided by GCI, Sergeant Berkley, and his operator Sergeant Carr, peering into his cathode tube, intercepted a Heinkel. Berkley fired a long burst, saw the unmistakable strikes of his De Wilde bullets, and for a few more fleeting seconds watched the Heinkel diving until it was swallowed up in the night. Another inconclusive combat. James Wheeler and Charles Maton — thanks as ever to the magic of GCI and AI — found and did battle with a Ju 88, but their discomfort at being held in the searchlights as they came into range was increased by a stream of tracer from the enemy. James fired and saw the flashes of his De Wilde on the Junkers, which dived away smartly and disappeared. One more enemy aircraft damaged.

While the GCI and AI were regularly working the miracle of guiding us to within sighting distance of a black bomber in the dark, the ensuing combat, so often inconclusive, began to weary and frustrate us. The enemy was hit — that could be seen by the flash of the De Wilde bullets as they struck — but he was not hit hard enough. Paddy Hemingway, however (his operator was the Australian Bailey, more at home at his radar set than as third man in my own Havoc) managed to strike a decisive blow, despite the blinding flash of his guns, on an unidentified enemy bomber. Its final plunge into the sea was confirmed by the Observer Corps.

Our commander-in-chief, Sholto Douglas, had most kindly invited me to call him direct at Fighter Command Headquarters if I had problems. I had already done so on a number of occasions, thereby incurring the displeasure of his technical staff officers. Throughout April I had pleaded with him to send us flash-eliminators for our guns. Even more insistently, I begged him to have our Havocs fitted with 20 mm cannons. This he promised to do as soon as possible.

It was already May, and the squadron moved thirty miles south to a new airfield, Hunsdon, with long, brand-new asphalt runways still smelling of fresh tar. During the first week of the month four more combats followed, two ending with the enemy 'probably destroyed', two classed as 'damaged'. Since October 1940 we had spent six months groping blindly for the enemy in the dark, with but one successful combat. In the past four weeks, with Havocs, AI and GCI, we had downed two of the enemy, with four 'probables' and six damaged. For the fourth month in succession we topped the list of 'night hours flown'. We had all tried, and felt certain at last that we were on our way to attaining that standard set by our one-time commander-in-chief Dowding, who on the very eve of our conversion from day to night-fighters had vowed that Fighter Command would never rest 'until we can locate, pursue and shoot down the enemy by day and by night'. By night we were not yet there, but things were slowly improving.

During the first nights of May the Luftwaffe, having failed for months in their attempts to subdue Liverpool and Glasgow, came back repeatedly as if in a last desperate attempt to have done with the job. Their blows fell too on Belfast and Barrow-in-Furness. On the 8th they struck out wildly at Nottingham, Hull and Sheffield. Together with other squadrons, we were able to help parry these blows. On the 9th we patrolled as usual, but no enemy came to tarnish the moonlight which illumined Britain that night. A silent night like that had often presaged in the past a coming storm.

25

THE LUFTWAFFE WITHDRAWS TO THE RUSSIAN FRONT

Indeed, the Luftwaffe were preparing, on the personal orders of Hitler, for exactly what they did not know. Although their losses of night-bombers were higher than ever — 190 aircrew killed or captured in April — they, or at least the younger ones, still believed in the invasion of Britain and thereafter victory. The older ones, less sanguine, when captured were only too glad to be out of the war. Those on active service were sustained meanwhile by the appeal of passing pleasures. On them and on the corpses of their comrades washed up on our shores were found cinema tickets or entry cards to this or that brothel. Such distractions helped to divert their thoughts from the nightmare of dying in the darkness over Britain. So too, once their course was set for England, did their emergency foods sustain them: choco-cola, which fortified the system and boosted the blood circulation; coffee beans, real ones, unavailable back in the Fatherland, which stimulated the nerves. Peppermint helped to slake their thirst, and 'Pervertine' kept them wide awake. And chewing-gum — there was nothing so good for soothing the nerves. On our side we did not resort to such artificial stimulants, least of all to chewing-gum. We were stimulated enough by the desire to defend our island. Not that I particularly desired to kill anyone; I just wanted to shoot out of our dark sky those black bombers which came to trouble and murder our people.

The German airmen felt surer of victory than did we, who were thinking more of survival. So sure were they that in their letters home they told their family and friends to send no more parcels. They would be back home before the present arrived. Yet none could deny that the strain of night operations was telling on them. Letters from home added to their anxieties; in the past they used to tell of laughable little British bombs falling here and there; now they related their accuracy and their devastating effect. Gas warfare remained a spectre in the minds of many a Luftwaffe airman; anti-gas defences in Germany were so lamentable that Germany might well get the worst of it. What most of them did not know was that the Luftwaffe was well armed in offensive gas weapons: gas bombs filled with lung gas, nasal irritants and nerve gas, and that the Wehrmacht, in readiness for invasion, was as well, if not better, equipped.

In a more local context, German air-crews were by now only too painfully aware of the increasing threat to their own lives from the British air defences in general, and night-fighters in particular, not to speak of the traps laid to catch them — the radio jammers 'Aspirin', 'Bromide' and 'Domino', those false beacons called 'Meacons' and 'Starfish', the decoy fires. But as brave soldiers of the Reich they flew on in the face of these embarrassing devices.

Another factor, more insidious, came to trouble their minds. Disturbing stories were circulating about Russia, Germany's ally for the past two years. Rumour had it that, incredibly, the alliance was about to break up and that Germany and the Soviet Union were on the verge of hostilities. Captured Luftwaffe men were beginning to wonder whether Germany could ever win the war. So far their apprehensions were the issue of vague imaginings, but the facts, unknown to them as yet, were on record.

As long ago as July 1940 Hitler had decided to invade Russia. When General Jodl confided the secret to officers of the High Command staff they were amazed. As long as Britain remained undefeated it was unthinkable that Germany should fight simultaneously on two fronts. Notwithstanding, planning for the Russian invasion began in October 1940. On 18 December the Fuehrer, in his Directive No. 21, had ordered that the German armed forces were to 'crush Soviet Russia in a quick campaign before the end of the war with England'. He and his sycophantic generals gave themselves six to eight weeks to complete the operation, code-named Barbarossa. The starting date was given as 15 May. But the defeat of the Italian armies in North Africa, and then in Greece, and Yugoslavia's spirited defiance — all of them forcing Hitler to intervene — diverted him from his dream of annihilating Russia and obliged him to postpone the invasion date to 22 June, a five weeks' delay which was to prove fatal.

The most astonishing feature in the Russian affair, after Hitler's duplicity, was Stalin's stupidity. The Soviet leader on 20 March 1941 was informed by the US Ambassador in Moscow of Hitler's planned invasion. Churchill too on 3 April tried to warn Stalin through the British Ambassador, Sir Stafford Cripps. Stalin gave no signs of alarm. On the contrary, Russian deliveries to Germany had risen 'by leaps and bounds' during March, according to a report from the German embassy in Moscow. In mid-April, at a farewell ceremony to the visiting Japanese Ambassador at Moscow station Stalin summoned the German Ambassador, Count Fritz von der Schulenberg, and before the assembled crowd of diplomats embraced him, saying: 'We must remain friends.' To the German military attaché, Colonel Krebs, he promised: 'We will remain friends with you through thick and thin.' Although a week later the Soviets were complaining to Berlin about Luftwaffe aircraft over-flying their border territory, they remained conciliatory. 'We shall not mind so long as it doesn't happen too often' was in effect their reply. By 24 April the British Ambassador, Cripps, was openly forecasting 22 June as the date of the German invasion. It was only on 30 April that Hitler secretly confirmed this date to his High Command.

At the beginning of May, in Moscow, rumours were rife of an imminent German invasion. They reached the ears of Stalin, of course, and worried him, as did reports of German forces massing on Russia's eastern frontier. But despite the warnings by the

US and Britain he refused to associate these ominous portents with the diabolical plans of Hitler. Stalin believed, in his ignorance, in lasting friendship between the Soviet Union and Germany. He was determined that there should be no conflict between the two countries. In the meantime the massing of German troops continued on Russia's frontiers and the Kriegsmarine took up their war dispositions.

Rommel's counter-attack on 31 March at El Agheila, some 150 miles by road west of Benghazi, marked the beginning of a disastrous period for Britain. Misled by first estimates of the enemy strength, Churchill three days later was not taking the threat too seriously. He wrote to Wavell about 'chopping' the enemy's advance and a 'rebuff' to the Germans; he could not believe that there was a 'persistent weight' behind Rommel's attack. 'If this blob could be cut off you may have a prolonged easement.' On the other hand, 'if they succeed in wandering onward, they will gradually destroy the effect of your victories.'

That was exactly what Rommel was about to do. As the British and Australians began falling back to Benghazi some 150 miles away, Wavell soon realized that Rommel's forces were stronger and swifter than he had supposed. In a despatch to Churchill he made a pathetic reference to his weakness in armour. One armoured division had in fact only one armoured brigade; thanks to the poor mechanical condition of his tanks, many had broken down. He could for the moment produce no more armour — much of it was in Greece. Churchill had told Wavell, 'A serious retreat beyond Benghazi would be melancholy.' Now Wavell had given orders for demolitions in that port, and evacuation began on 4 April. Two days later the British and Australians were in full retreat. The Australians defending Tobruk beat off two attacks and earned a message from Churchill 'Bravo Tobruk.' But the enemy, leaving the port aside for the time being, pressed on eastward in the direction of Egypt. On 12 April they took Bardia, a few miles from the Egyptian frontier, where, their men exhausted and their lines of communication extended to the limit, they halted. Rommel, the Desert Fox, had achieved a brilliant operation; for the British, in

Churchill's words, it was a disaster of the first magnitude. They were back where they had started in December.

He now directed the Royal Navy to intervene with all their might to impede the enemy. They must cut his communications from Italy and Sicily to Rommel's supply port Tripoli, using surface craft, submarines and aircraft — 'Heavy losses in battleships, cruisers and destroyers must if necessary be accepted', the 'Former Naval Person' added grimly, and again. 'Every enemy convoy which gets through must be considered a serious naval failure.' Tripoli must be bombarded from the sea, so also must the coastal road leading eastward to Egypt. As well, German transport along this vital road must be ceaselessly harassed by commandos and other forces landed from the sea or in sallies from Tobruk. Here again losses must be faced. 'The urgency is extreme', Churchill insisted, 'especially should the German attack on Yugoslavia and Greece succeed.' At that moment, in mid-April, it showed every likelihood of doing so.

The German Twelfth Army had crossed the frontiers of Yugoslavia and Greece on 6 April. While Yugoslav resistance gradually collapsed the Greek armies, though stiffened by 53,000 British troops from North Africa, were falling back before the overwhelming numbers of the Wehrmacht and the Luftwaffe. Churchill, harking back to the glory of ancient Greece, envisaged a last heroic stand at Thermopylae, but the Greek army, after months of heroic resistance, were no longer in a position to support the British.

Wavell thereupon ordered the re-embarkation of his troops — British, Australian and New Zealanders. As at Dunkirk, so now on the beaches of Greece, the Royal Navy and the Allied merchant fleet with the habitual calm and skill performed a heroic feat. With the Luftwaffe undisputed masters of the air, evacuation could only proceed by dark. During five successive nights the sailors brought off some 42,000 men; more than half of them were taken to Crete, where the final act of the Greek tragedy would be played. Nearly 12,000 soldiers were lost in Greece; twenty-six vessels, including 21 Greek (five of them hospital ships), were sunk during the evacuation.

British participation in the Greek campaign was more an act of *noblesse oblige* than a response to a binding obligation. It touched people in the United States, and not least the President, who wrote to Churchill: 'You have done not only heroic but very useful work in Greece . . .' and then went on to express, in rather over-simplified terms, his confidence in Britain's victory in the Mediterranean and the Middle East.

On 4 May Churchill in his reply was in sombre mood. 'We shall fight on, whatever happens' he told Roosevelt, and begged him to remember that the final outcome of the struggle might well depend on present events in the Mediterranean. If Europe, much of Asia and Africa became part of the Axis system, that would mean 'a hard, long and bleak struggle' by Britain, the Commonwealth and the United States. Meanwhile, wrote Churchill, the British were determined to fight to the last inch and ounce for Egypt, Tobruk and Crete. 'I adjure you, Mr President', he concluded, 'not to underrate the gravity of the consequences which may follow from a Middle Eastern collapse. In this war, every post is a winning-post, and how many more are we going to lose?'

As Churchill was in the act of writing to Roosevelt, the German Fuehrer in Berlin was crowing over his latest victories; his speech was well-laced, as usual, with insults directed at Churchill: 'The most bloodthirsty and amateurish strategist in history. . . . As a soldier he is a bad politician and as a politician an equally bad soldier.' Hitler ended by suggesting that Churchill's 'abnormal' state of mind could only be explained as symptomatic either of a paralytic disease or of a drunkard's ravings. It was a pathetic performance, particularly as the Nazi war-lord himself was about to make the biggest strategic blunder of his life. Despite the attempts by some of his advisers to dissuade him, his land-locked mind was incapable of appreciating the awful predicament of Britain in the Mediterranean and on its shores, not to mention the Atlantic. Instead, he remained obsessed with his plan to invade Russia before turning, 'in six or eight weeks' as he had said, to rend Britain at this point at the nadir of her fortunes.

Churchill was the only man living who had the measure of this wicked, vainglorious and foolish man. In sober, measured terms the British prime minister had the previous day spoken to the nation in that very personal way he had of moving us to the core of our being. After the recent disasters in Europe and North Africa 'we must not', he said, 'lose our sense of proportion and thus become discouraged or alarmed. When we face with a steady eye the difficulties which lie before us, we may derive new confidence from remembering those we have already overcome.' He went on to quote two verses of the Victorian poet Arthur Hugh Clough which, he said, 'seem apt and appropriate to our fortunes tonight, and I believe they will be so judged wherever the English language is spoken or the flag of freedom flies.' With millions of others, I was listening intently. At this moment of our great tribulation the words of the prime minister and the poet fell superb and sweet on the ear.

> For while the tired waves, vainly breaking,
>   Seem here no painful inch to gain,
> Far back, through creeks and inlets making,
>   Comes silent, flooding in, the main.
>
> And not by eastern windows only,
>   When daylight comes, comes in the light;
> In front the sun climbs slow, how slowly!
>   But westward, look, the land is bright.

26

THE WORM IN THE APPLE:
FLIGHT OF THE DEPUTY FUEHRER

Yet another disaster was impending. The Luftwaffe through March, April and May, backing up the U-boats, sank 179 ships. In early May 40,000 tons were destroyed in the docks of Liverpool -- that 'tormented target'. The offensive against the ports had reached its climax; after another heavy assault on Belfast and Glasgow, the Luftwaffe came back to London on the night of 10 May.

The idea for the raid occurred during a boring and seemingly interminable tea party hosted by Hitler for a bunch of his cronies at his mountain retreat, the Berghof, in the Bavarian Alps. It was Martin Bormann, Hitler's bull-necked private secretary, who raised the subject: the RAF had once again bombed Berlin. How about another reprisal raid on London? Orders went out to General Hugo Sperrle, the fleshy, sadistic commander-in-chief of Luftlotte 3, at his headquarters in the Hôtel Luxembourg in Paris. 'Target London: all available aircraft.' That meant five hundred or so, for a large reserve was already held back in preparation for 'Barbarossa'. Sperrle in 1937, during the Spanish Civil War, had planned the attack on Guernica, which killed thousands of civilians. London could expect no quarter in this special reprisal attack. Yet if Sperrle's motto was 'Is there a foe that bombing cannot break?' London would give him a positive answer.

Targets were allotted: the Victoria Docks opposite Woolwich; West Ham, Stepney, Millwall Docks and the West India Docks, and finally Battersea Power Station. Kampfgeschwader 100 was to lead the attack with incendiaries, but since the Luftwaffe meteo men ('weather frogs' as they were called) had forecast clear visibility under a full moon, they would not need their X-Gerät for the actual bombing — just as well, for British 'Domino' jamming sent it haywire. But the beam from Cherbourg was laid on all the same; it cut the intersecting beam from Holland over West Ham. By 6 p.m. Fighter Command, AA Command and the Fire Service Headquarters at Lambeth had all been informed. What deeply concerned the firemen was that the Thames that night would be at ebb-tide. Pump suction hoses lowered from Thames bridges might not reach the water; from the river embankment firemen would have to carry them across twenty yards of slimy, stinking mud before they could be immersed in the river.

Across the Channel in the Pas de Calais, around 6 p.m. Oberstleutnant Adolf ('Dolfo') Galland, commanding 26 Jagdgeschwader, received an unexpected call from Göring in Berlin. Galland was to get his fighters into the air immediately. 'But Herr Reichsmarschall', Galland dared to object, 'there are no enemy bombers flying in.' 'I'm not talking about aircraft flying in', bellowed the Reichsmarschall, 'I'm asking you to stop one flying out — and shoot it down!' A few minutes later half a dozen of Galland's Messerschmitt 109s were in the air searching for the mysterious aircraft. By 7.30 p.m. they had all landed back at their base with nothing to report.

Three hours later — and by British double summer-time the sky, with a rising moon, still glowed with light — eleven of Kampfgruppe 100's Heinkels were heading across the Channel on their X-Gerät for London. By now the south and east coast radar stations were saturated with plots, duly reproduced in the operations map at Fighter Command where our commander-in-chief Sholto Douglas gravely surveyed the attack massing on London. As the enemy converged on the capital Sholto was puzzled by a single plot crossing the North Sea not far from the

English coast and travelling considerably faster than the bombers. It crossed the coast near Alnwick in Northumberland at 10.23 p.m. A few minutes later the Observer Corps post at Chatton, near Edinburgh, reported having sighted the aircraft flying low — a Messerschmitt 110. Impossible, replied the controller at Fighter Command — a Me 100 could never get that far and return to base. He ordered a fighter up to intercept, but the plot, heading north-east, faded. It was about 10.45 p.m.

A couple of minutes after 11 p.m. KGr. 100 was over West Ham, where in moonlight nearly as bright as day they bombed visually, opening an attack such as London had never yet endured. Unlike the great fire raid of 29 December, which was concentrated on the square mile of the City around St Paul's, the deluge of high-explosive and incendiary bombs spread, during the next five hours to the heart of the City and northward to Shoreditch; to St Marylebone, Paddington, Kensington and Battersea in the west, and south of the river, to Bermondsey, Deptford, Greenwich and Lewisham. Fire and destruction rained down without discrimination — on Lambeth Palace, where the archbishop was in residence, on the sick and dying in St Thomas's hospital; fires raged at Waterloo station, St Pancras and Paddington, consumed the roofs of the thousand-year old Abbey of Westminster, of Westminster Hall and the House of Lords; the chamber of the House of Commons was gutted. The Old Bailey, Gray's Inn Hall and five Wren churches were among scores of historic buildings shattered by blast and fire. Faraday House, nerve centre of London's telephone system, and St Paul's cathedral, surrounded by flames, were threatened for hours. Hundreds of private dwellings suffered the same fate, their owners imploring the fire-fighters to save their property and belongings instead of trying to rescue buildings which belonged to the ancient past.

The crying problem was water. No less than 600,000 gallons a minute were needed to extinguish the conflagrations which raged in the one square mile of the City alone. The Thames at low tide could not provide enough; the 5000-gallon static tanks sited here and there in the streets ran dry. Some pumps searched for water in the sewers of London, only to find the filters of their pumps were soon clogged with detritus. That night the Luftwaffe lit over 2200 separate fires.

In the midst of this inferno, near the Royal Mint, a few streets away from the Tower of London, Chief Fire Officer Alfred Shawyer was instructing the pumps as they drove up. Shawyer, six feet tall and solidly built, had been a prize-fighter before the war, and had fought for Britain in the Golden Gloves tournament in New York. In his off-hours he had become a keen ball-room dancer — under the tutelage of no other than Johnny Callow. In the mid-thirties the two had become good friends, but in time their ways had separated.

At this moment Johnny's No. 1 Pump, accompanied by No. 6, was heading for the conflagration in central London. When the bells had gone down at the sub-station the order was 'The Minories!' 'Where the hell's that?' Johnny asked his driver Fred Cosh. 'I'll show you', replied Fred; a cockney, he knew the City like the back of his hand. Driving flat out up the Old Kent Road, he came to the Bricklayer's Arms and turned right, dodging through narrow streets until he reached London Bridge. Before they were half-way across Johnny began sniffing the air. 'What's that terrible smell?' he asked Fred. 'Oh, shut up, Johnny!' shouted Fred. 'That's Billingsgate Fish Market. Round here I follow me nose.' Past the fish-market they sped, then had to pick their way down small streets strewn with debris, sometimes having to back and find another way among the crashing bombs and roaring fires. At last Fred came to a halt. 'Here we are, the Minories, and next door to the Royal Mint. Plenty of money in there for us, Johnny!' he chuckled.

Johnny got down from the car and, on heel and toe — his dancer's step — he strode toward the red-and-white checked control van and confronted the control officer to ask for instructions. But instead he blurted out: 'Blimey, Alf, if it isn't you!' and Alf Shawyer with a great laugh exclaimed, 'Blimey, Johnny, it's been five years. What a place to meet again!' It was neither the place nor the time for reminiscences. Johnny and his men unrolled their hoses, found a hydrant and connected up. For the

203

next four hours, under ceaseless bombardment and with barely enough water pressure, they fought the fire until it died. Alf Shawyer told Johnny, 'Better knock off now, mate. Tata, see you later!' 'You bet!' shouted Johnny and drove off.

Badly mauled though the surrounding boroughs of Greenwich, Deptford and Lewisham were, Woolwich received but one serious hit — once again on the long-suffering Arsenal, where high explosives and incendiaries kept firemen and rescue squads busy all night. Johnny's young brother Ray did less running than usual that night, but was proud to be on duty when the London sirens sounded for the 545th time in the last nine months.

When, after seven hours of bombardment the all-clear sounded at 6 a.m., London was still burning, and smouldered on for several days. Its citizens were left to mourn nearly 1500 dead and pray for thousands of injured.

War, since it existed, has been associated with massacres of the civil population. But after 'this hellish invention', as Churchill had called it, of air warfare the massacre of innocents was being perpetrated, on an ever-increasing scale, not by the drunken, dastard soldiery of yore who slew and pillaged with impunity, but, despite themselves, by sober young airmen of rare courage. The paradox was a cruel one.

Night-fighters were up in force all through that night, which Fighter Command had declared, for reasons of moon and visibility, a 'Fighter Night'. Cats-eye fighters, Hurricanes, Spitfires and Defiants 'stacked up' over London, Beachy Head (on the Sussex coast) and other strategic points, reported many sightings and combats. Between them they claimed nineteen enemy bombers destroyed. AA guns, their shooting restricted by the Fighter Night rules to a height of 12,000 feet, claimed to have downed four more. The specialized radar night-fighters, better suited to darker nights, when they could stalk the enemy unseen, shot down another four. Alas, the claim of 27 enemy aircraft destroyed later proved to be wildly exaggerated. The Luftwaffe lost only eight aircraft that night. Of these, two were certainly accounted for by 85 Squadron.

First off from Hunsdon were Flight Lieutenant Gordon Raphael and his operator Sergeant Addison. Gordon, a hardy, ascetic Canadian, suffered neither fools nor Germans gladly. With the burning city visible from Hunsdon, Gordon was in high dudgeon when, after preliminary directions from GCI and skilful guidance by Addison, he sighted a Heinkel 111. With no time to lose lest the Heinkel see him, he closed in fast, his bead on the bomber's left engine — it was Gordon's private theory that hitting one power unit and the wing tanks gave better results. Tonight he proved his theory. The stricken Heinkel spiralled down steeply to the left, caught fire and exploded before crashing.

85's second victory was scored by Flying Officer Evans with Sergeant Carter as operator, an unassuming but throughly professional pair. The procedure GCI to AI to visual went smoothly, and Evans (though his Havoc presented a fine target in the moonlight) was not spotted by the enemy, a Heinkel, whose engines and fuselage he sprayed from short range. Evans's technique too was deadly. The Heinkel pitched forward and, streaming sparks, went down in a dive so steep that the Havoc could not follow. The German plane was already half consumed by flames before hitting the ground. The time was 2.30 in the morning of the 11th.

While, at the summons of ground control, the Havocs of my squadron roared down the runway and up into the night I myself — for reasons I shall soon explain — remained unusually passive on the ground. From our dispersal point at Hunsdon we could see the immense, incandescent glow which rose above London, staining blood-red the fair moonlit sky. From where we watched, sixty miles north of the capital, it was an awful sight.

And while, all through that fiery night, the hundreds of enemy bombers bore down on London, saturating our coastal radar screens, Fighter Command control watched, mystified, the plots of a lone aircraft flying northward, out to sea. Later, it turned inland and the plots disappeared near Glasgow. At Bonnyton, north of that city, a crofter, David McLean, saw an aircraft crash and burst into flames; above, in their glare, a man was visible, swinging on the end of a parachute. Some minutes later, back in his cottage, David was offering tea to the shaken pilot. A German, handsome with dark eyes and bushy eyebrows, he told McLean that his name was Albert Horn, *hauptmann* in the Luftwaffe. Later at the Central Police Station in Glasgow, the German gave a different name: Rudolf Hess.

If that were true the man standing in the police station was no ordinary Luftwaffe pilot but the deputy Fuehrer of the Third Reich and Hitler's right-hand man. He asked to see Wing Commander the Duke of Hamilton, at present commanding the Turnhouse (Edinburgh) sector.

'Douglo' Hamilton, a shy and sparely built man with straight blond hair, was instructed by the Commander-in-Chief, Fighter Command, to go over to Glasgow. There the Duke was convinced that the German was indeed Rudolf Hess. He had come to Britain, he said, to discuss a peace plan.

Winston Churchill, as was so often his wont, had been spending the week-end at the house of Mr and Mrs Ronald Tree at Ditchley, near Oxford. Throughout dinner the progress of that Saturday night's fire raid on London had been telephoned to him from the Home Security War Room. Dinner over, the guests were enjoying a movie. *The Marx Brothers go West*, when the prime minister's secretary, Miss Shearburn, came and whispered to him, 'I have a very urgent message for you.' Churchill, absorbed by the antics of the Marx Brothers, did not budge for a few minutes. Then he left his seat to read the message which had been typed out on a slip of paper. It read 'Rudolf Hess has arrived in Scotland.' Churchill took the paper, glanced at it, then looked up, beaming, and said: 'The worm is in the apple.'

The reason why, that night, I had not taken off on patrol with the rest was that the 11 Group Commander, Air Vice Marshal Leigh-Mallory, had insisted a month previously that I take it easy. Despite my own impulsive feelings, I had respected his advice; I knew he was right. I was completely whacked — I believe the Luftwaffe had their own word, *ausflugen*, out-flown, flown to a standstill. As a pilot, I was no longer functioning properly; while the spirit was still willing, the flesh and its vital functions of vision and reflex were weak. That half-hour-long, inconclusive combat with the Junkers 88 in early April was to me a disturbing sign, but one that I was not prepared to admit. On the other hand, when Leigh-Mallory had granted me another two months with the Squadron, I already knew I was dead-beat. I suspect he did too, for he had known me ever since, nearly a year ago, I had been given command of 85 Squadron.

When shot down for the second time at the end of August 1940 I was already nearing the end of my tether. Otherwise I should never have rushed headlong into that swarm of Messerschmitts knowing full well that they were bound to get me. Air fighting, like any other, may need courage, but it requires too intelligence and even prudence, as the great First World War German ace Manfred von Richthofen proved when at the height of his career he was killed because of forgetting that rule. The longer you kept fighting, the more you needed cunning rather than just plain dash and derring-do.

In air combat, skill alone — this I had acquired in nearly two years of day- and night-fighting — is not enough. Luck played a big part. I had enjoyed more than my fair share, ever since those first combats in early 1940. Time after time my aircraft had been hit; bullets had holed the wings and fuselage, they had zipped through the propeller past my head, between my legs even. One had exploded in the cockpit, bringing me down in the sea, yet unhurt; another had hit me, downing me once more. Luck — I would dare say God — had helped me survive the perils of the night, the cruel weather and the enemy combined.

Not that, oddly enough, any of these things had particularly frightened me. In fighters, even night-fighters, we had our own way of enjoying the funny side of danger, however hideous, and laughing at each other's stories over a pint or two of beer. But the trouble was that these hair-raising experiences accumulated to form stress, a word we ourselves only knew in its aerodynamic context, as applied to our beloved aircraft. But we too, our minds and bodies and nervous systems, were, without our noticing it under increasing stress, which if not relieved in time would break us and plunge us into the dark, deep pit of depression and fear. Against them there was but one antidote, action. But action, like a drug, made such demands on the body that we came to living on our nerves alone. That was the beginning of the end.

In my case (there were hundreds of others) Leigh-Mallory, in his wisdom, had noticed this. He prescribed less action. Our medical officer had noticed too; he put me on barbiturates which were supposed to calm the nerves and induce sleep. But my body, hardened for months against fatigue and insomnia, fought the drug, which only made me feel worse.

As indeed did the reduced dose of action, which left me failing as a pilot, and a night-fighter pilot at that. I was no longer the pilot I had been. But I had been given a stay of command until mid-June. I must hold out till then, not overdoing it as was my habit, through pride or just plain foolishness, but taking my normal turn to patrol.

Unexpectedly, the nights were henceforth quiet; apart from a few sporadic raids the Luftwaffe simply vanished in the darkness. The 'blitz' was over. Britain had thwarted Hitler's declared intention — to eliminate her as a base for continuing the war. This she remained until the end, when his tyranny was overthrown.

27

EPILOGUE:
THE END OF THE LONG, DARK NIGHT

With *der Tag*, D-Day for Hitler's attack on Russia, fixed for 22 June the Luftwaffe after their final blitz on London were hastily transferring the majority of their units from the British to the Russian front. Thanks to the Germans' failure to 'annihilate' Russia, the Luftwaffe did not return within the six to eight weeks envisaged by Hitler to finish off Britain. The enemy's pressure on the home front subsided and remained negligible for the next twenty months.

Meanwhile the Greek campaign culminated in disaster when the Germans overran Crete at the end of May. In the Atlantic the Royal Navy and the RAF were gradually gaining the upper hand. On 27 May the Navy and its Air Arm sank the so-called unsinkable *Bismarck*, all set to prey on the Atlantic convoys. By July the worst of the Atlantic battle was over. The Japanese attack on Pearl Harbour on 7 December brought the Americans into the Pacific war. But it would be months before the tide of war turned, in 1942, against the Germans, with the Russian victory before Stalingrad and the British offensive at El Alamein in North Africa.

The last attack on London was, as Churchill affirmed, the worst. Had there been many more of that intensity London, through sheer exhaustion of her civil defence resources, might well have been unable to 'take it' any longer. But London had made it — so had every other British city. A popular ditty, sung by those lovable Cockney comedians Flanagan and Allen, went:

> We've won it, we've done
> We've beaten them at last
> Up in the air . . .

'Down on the ground' would have been a truer line.

All the same, our night defences had increased immeasurably in strength since August 1940, and in all sectors. In the Wizard War we had sown confusion among the enemy, as we had done with rather less refined means, with 'Starfish' sites. Our anti-aircraft guns and searchlights no longer amused the enemy night-bombers with their harmless firework displays; they were now recognized as a real menace. Our night-fighter squadrons were regularly clawing the enemy out of the night sky; not that eight out of five hundred downed on that night of 10 May was anything like the hiding we gave them during the day battle in 1940. But Sholto Douglas was confident that with further aids our night-fighters would get the better of them. Thank God, for London and the rest of Britain's cities, his theory was not put to the test.

85 Squadron, which had grown up, not without pain, from cats-eye fighters to AI fighters, kept on with their good work. I made my last patrol with them early in June, then departed to join the night operations staff at No. 11 Group.

My successor was a likeable, debonair and moustachioed stranger, 'Scruffy' Saunders. Alas, he stayed with them only four months until he and his operator, Pilot Officer Austin, were shot down during a night combat over the North Sea. A similar fate put an end to the young lives of Sergeant Berkley and his operator Sergeant Carr over the Thames estuary. Following 'Scruffy', No. 85 passed into the capable hands of Gordon Raphael until in 1943 John Cunningham (still teamed with his operator Jimmy Rawnsley) took his place and led the squadron, now equipped with the sensational De Havilland Mosquito, on to battle with enemy night-bombers (and night-fighters too) over their own territory.

It was in April 1943, as 'station-master' at West Malling, a day and night fighter base in Kent, that I finally got even with that Heinkel which had landed at Debden and escaped. Our resident night-fighter squadron, No. 29, had been operating against lightning raiders, single-seater Focke-Wulf 190s which climbed high over France, dived down on London and loosed off one or two bombs. Towards midnight the sector controller called me in the control tower: 'All is quiet now; you can relax.' I returned to my room in the mess and lay on my bed, but this time fully clothed − in case. Ten minutes later an aircraft with an odd exhaust note passed low overhead. I called the duty officer, 'Curly' Clay (he was quite bald), and asked him 'What's that aircraft that has just landed?' A moment later he reported 'It's one of ours.' 'Curly', I said, 'Please take another look.' This time he came back to the telephone and in a voice which had risen several octaves stammered, 'It's a Focke-Wulf 190!' 'Grab it!' I told him. 'I'll be with you in a minute.'

When I arrived at the control tower I found, parked on the tarmac, a black Focke-Wulf 190. In the control room on the first floor stood a German pilot, and on each side of him one of our men pointing a bayonet at his tummy. In the minute or so before I had arrived the little Hillman van in which sat two girls of the WAAF (Women's Auxiliary Air Force) had driven out to the aircraft, which had stopped on the flare-path. They had believed it to be one of our returning bombers. Just in front of it the driver turned and switched on the illuminated panel on the roof which said FOLLOW ME. This the German did, comprehending nothing. As he reached the tarmac and switched off the AA liaison officer climbed on to the Focke-Wulf's wing and, short of a revolver, stuck a pencil into the pilot's back and said something resembling *'Hände hoffen'*, hands up. Thus was thirty-year-old Feldwebel Otto Bechte taken prisoner.

In another room on the first floor of the control tower I listened as our interrogator questioned him, without understanding a word apart from his repeated reply *'Ich bin ein Deutsche soldat'*. Suddenly the door was flung open and Paul Arbon (who happened to be there − I cannot remember why) announced,

breathless: 'There's another one just landed!' With Paul following I spun, hardly touching the steps, down the spiral staircase,
and ran outside just in time to see the 'Beaverette' — a small
armoured car — driving off towards the Focke-Wulf, which was
still on the flare-path, its propeller turning. I yelled after them
'Don't shoot!', to be answered by a sharp burst of machine-gun
fire. In a moment the Focke-Wulf was on fire; the pilot, on fire too,
was climbing down from the cockpit when Paul and I arrived. We
leapt on him, knocked him to the ground, beat out the flames of
his burning flying-suit, and dragged him away from his aircraft.
As it blazed, the flames fanned by the still revolving propeller, our
firemen were playing their foam hoses on it. The German pilot
meanwhile, still on the ground, yelled and struggled like a mad-
man so that Paul and I had to use all our strength to hold him
down. Then suddenly, in a gigantic explosion, the Focke-Wulf
disintegrated, badly injuring two of our firemen with splinters.
The rest went over the top of our heads as we knelt on the German.

A little later, during his interrogation, I asked why he was making such a fuss, lying there on the ground, and he answered 'I was
trying to tell that idiot' — pointing at me — that there was a 50-kilo
bomb still in my aircraft.' Oberleutnant Heinz Setzer thought he
was in France, and took me for a Frenchman.

The curtain had not yet fallen on this drama. A bobby appeared
and informed me 'There's another one down half a mile short of
the runway!' I drove with him through the dark lanes and came to
a farmhouse surrounded by orchards. Inside sat a German pilot,
badly injured about the head, drinking tea with a bewildered
elderly couple. Oberfeldwebel Otto Schultz, seeing the West
Malling flare-path, had tried to pull off an emergency landing.
The lights went out at the last moment, and Schultz crashed into
the apple-trees. He, like his comrades, had lost himself comletely
in the hazy weather, and believed he was in France.

In hospital Schultz showed me a photo of his pretty wife and
two lovely fair-haired children. What a sad mess the world was in
— and it was less than five years since my first night flight in the
peaceful, starry sky of Singapore.

BIBLIOGRAPHY

Blake, Lewis, *Red Alert* (Published by the Author, London, 1982).

Brookes, Andrew J., *Fighter Squadron at War* (Ian Allan, London).

Clayton, Aileen, *The Enemy is Listening* (Ballantine Books, New York, 1982).

Collier, Basil, *The Defence of the United Kingdom* (HMSO, London, 1957).

Collier, Richard, *The City that would not die* (E. P. Dutton, New York, 1960).

Churchill, Winston S., *The Second World War, Volume I* (Cassell, London, 1948).

Churchill, Winston S., *Their Finest Hour* (Houghton Mifflin, Boston, 1949).

Churchill, Winston S., *The Second World War, Volume III* (Cassell, London, 1950).

His Majesty's Stationery Office, *London: Front Line 1940–1941* (Published 1942).

Horley, Ronald T., *Occurrences 1939–45* (Private Memoirs – By kind permission of Patrick Langrishe).

Kee, Robert and Smith, Joanna, *We'll Meet Again* (Dent, London, 1984).

Price, Alfred, *Instruments of Darkness* (William Kimber, London, 1967).

Rawnsley C. F. and Wright, Robert, *Night Fighter* (Collins, London, 1957; Corgi Books, 1959).

Richards, Denis, *Royal Air Force 1939–45. Volume I* (HMSO, London, 1953).

Shirer, William L., *The Rise and Fall of the Third Reich* (Pan Books, London, 1964).

Stahl, Peter W., *The Diving Eagle* (William Kimber, London, 1984).

Terraine, John, *The Right of the Line* (Hodder and Stoughton, London, 1985).

Wakefield, Kenneth, *The First Pathfinders* (William Kimber, London, 1981).

Wallington, Neil, *Fireman!* (David and Charles, London, 1979).

—— , *Firemen at War* (David and Charles, London, 1981).

Wood, Derek, and Dempster, Derek, *The Narrow Margin* (Hutchinson, London, 1961).

INDEX

Ranks are given where known. These are as obtaining at the time of the incidents described.

Schultz, Oberfeldwebel Otto, 212
Schulz, Werner, 160
Schutzstaffel (SS), 35
Sea Lion (Seelöwe), Operation, 56, 82
Searchlight Control Radar (SLC), 53, 159
Searchlights, 32, 41, 111, 159
Secret weapons, 39, 161, 176
Sector defence, of Fighter Command, 16
Seelöwe — see Sea Lion, Operation
Seilbombe, 176
Setzer, Oberleutnant Heinz, 212
Shawyer, Chief Fire Officer Alfred, 203, 204
Sheffield, raids on (December 1940), 139–40
Shirer, William, quoted, 51
Sidcot flying-suit, 154
Silvertown, 77
Simon, Lord, 190
Simpson, John, 41–2
Sinclair, Sir Archibald, secretary of state for air, 107–8, 115
Singapore, 11–14, 31, 41, 175
Sound-locators, 32
Sperrle, General Hugo, 65, 161, 200
Spitfire — see Supermarine Spitfire
Splittenbomben (fragmentation bombs), 109
Sprengbomben (high-explosive bombs), 109
Stainforth, Group Captain George, 163
Stalin, Marshal Joseph, 147, 195
Stalingrad, battle of, 191
Stammers, Warrant Officer, 169
'Starfish' (decoy fires), 62, 143, 173
Station 'X' — see Code and Cypher School

Steeple Morden (Beds), 158
Stollberg, Knickebein transmitter at, 50
Suffolk, Earl of, in bomb-disposal, 87–8
Sunderland raided, 190
Supermarine S.6, 163
Supermarine Spitfire, 28, 59, 64, 150, 204
Surrey Commercial Docks, 75
Swansea raided (February 1941), 152

Tanglin Club, Singapore, 12
Tangmere (Sussex) airfield, 15, 39, 40
Telecommunications Research Establishment (Swanage), 54, 100
Templecombe (Somerset), meacon at, 101, 123
Thompson, Fire Commander, 112–13
Tirpitz (pocket battleship), 145
Tobruk (Libya), 181, 196
Tower of London bombed, 142
Townsend, Michael, 85, 183
Townsend, Squadron Leader Peter: pre-war flying in Singapore, 12–14; in Hawker Furies in No. 43, 15–18; switched to Hurricanes, 29; first combat (3 February 1940), 42; takes command of No. 85 at Debden, 46; perils of night-flying, 47–8; injured in combat, 63; leaves hospital, 85; rejoins Squadron, 91; told to switch to night-fighting, 93; prangs, 126–7; moves to Gravesend, 129; reports Squadron ready for night-fighting, 184; instructed to